VIEWS FROM THE TIGHTROPE

MITCH BOBROW, MSW, has been a practicing psychotherapist for more than fifteen years. He helps
people turn their lives into daring adventures by using
risks wisely. He has also served as a workshop leader
and communications consultant for a variety of major
corporations. For information on programs he offers
for therapists, other professionals, and the general
public, contact Mitch by e-mail at Mitch@Baka.com
or on the web at Tightrope.baka.com.

VIEWS FROM THE TIGHTROPE

LIVING WISELY IN AN UNCERTAIN WORLD

MITCH BOBROW

PUBLISHED FOR THE PAUL BRUNTON
PHILOSOPHIC FOUNDATION BY

LARSON PUBLICATIONS

International Standard Book Number: 0-943914-84-1
Library of Congress Catalog Card Number: 97-74022

Published for the Paul Brunton Philosophic Foundation by
Larson Publications
4936 NYS Route 414
Burdett, NY 14818 USA

04 03 02 01 00 99 98 97

10 9 8 7 6 5 4 3 2 1

The quotation on page 86 is reprinted with permission of
HarperCollins Publishers from the Dalai Lama's foreword to
Thoughts without a Thinker, © 1995 by Mark Epstein, M.D.

The letter on page 157 is reprinted with permission
from its writer.

CONTENTS

Acknowledgments

I SHUDDER to think what this book would have looked like without the help of David Shalloway—the ultimate tightrope artist whose insistence on lucidity is only one of his many inspirational qualities.

To my publisher and editor, Paul Cash, I have much to be grateful for. First for his belief in me and the viability of this project. Second for his guiding hand in keeping me on purpose and bringing out my best. Lastly for his painstaking editorial help. Working with Paul has given me new appreciation of the old saying, "God is in the details."

I am grateful to Amy Opperman Cash, marketing director of Larson Publications, who from the start has believed in this work and has been a source of encouragement and good ideas. With the book done, the marketing fun begins.

My two older sons, Peter and Hilly, have pored over the manuscript and added many valuable suggestions while insisting that I not sound preachy. They are living proof that a college education is worth the investment. I'm glad I got something more than a bunch of A's in return for all the money their education cost. I have asked them to inspire me with their lives and they continually deliver.

My two younger children, Jake and Mikayla, supported me to have fun when I wasn't writing. They keep me in balance.

I am especially indebted to Gigi Marks, whose labor of love is deeply noted and whose contribution made this book better. Susan Savishinsky, Kelly Morris, Lindy Cummings, and David Mulveney also read sections of the manuscript and made valuable contributions.

A special thank-you to all the clients who have courageously shared their lives and who have opened their hearts to me.

The enthusiasm, love, and support provided by my sister and father continually uplift me. If I know something about unconditional love, I have my family members to thank.

Jack Kornfield has been my meditation teacher and role model for the past eleven years. His devotion and wisdom have lighted my way.

This book could not have been written without the blessing and support of my wife, Kathy. Not only did she consent to my sharing our relationship, she worked on the entire text—offering encouragement and wise counsel. Her commitment to being alive pervades my life and this work.

Identifying details have been changed to protect the anonymity of my clients.

INTRODUCTION

A T THE time I had been a single parent for more than a year. The nightmare of separation and divorce was fading. My family of three was turning into a well-functioning, happy unit. The hardest part was driving off to work before the two boys left for school—especially since they had to cross a state highway to catch their school bus. On this particular morning, Hilly, the eight-year-old, came jumping into my arms just as I was about to leave for work.

"Daddy, daddy," he exclaimed, "I just *have* to tell you how much I love you." His innocent, joyful smile radiated love as he hugged me tightly. Then, looking directly into my eyes he said it again: "I love you, daddy."

For a moment I just soaked up his effusive love and felt blessed to be the father of such a son. After the long hug, Hilly hopped down and went merrily off to finish his breakfast. Mulling over my good fortune, I skipped out gently towards my car. Then a strange and unexpected wave of intense emotion poured over me. I was startled by an upsurge of rage. Why should my son's spontaneous generosity so upset me?

Instead of driving away, I sat in the car for a while, curious and dazed. I felt angry at God—or was it life itself?—for the incredible uncertainty that clouds my existence. I had no guarantee that all would stay well and that each member of my family would be safe and alive hours later when I returned home from work.

Like everyone else's, my subconscious is full of horror stories of mutilated children and sudden, unexpected, family-destroying disasters. Hilly's overflowing warmth, which at first triggered love and gratitude, soon uncovered the terror and biting anger that I also live with. I shuddered at the thought of how unbearably empty my life would be without him.

A shadow of fragility and vulnerability now weighed heavy on my heart, replacing anger with sobriety.

At that moment, I realized I had a choice. I could hold back some of my love to protect myself; or I could accept the risks inherent in life—painful and terrifying as they are—and continue to love and give all of myself.

To live fully we must love deeply. Loving deeply requires a willing surrender to the unknown. It requires vulnerability. It means we must accept and work with risk.

Love stretches us to explore our limits. Love asks us to disappear into the moment where its glory is revealed and to have faith that we can bear whatever we must face. When we shy away from risk, then we simultaneously shy away from love. And if we shy away from love, we are no longer fully alive. We are called upon to love, to melt into each moment, to have faith that we will abide, all the while knowing that we don't know what lies ahead.

Deep down we all know this, but in our fear we slip into comfortable but unconscious habits that prevent us from tasting directly the true joy of life. Something blocks us from standing too close to the light and glory of our intense fragility.

Lord Krishna, one of the Hindu gods, was once asked by his chief disciple to describe the strangest thing about all of existence. Krishna replied that although we know intellectually that we will die and that death and decay are all about us, we never believe in our guts that it will happen to us. We ignore the essential, protecting ourselves in a thousand different ways from seeing the terrifying reality that our lives are transitory and can only be appreciated when we stop and cherish life itself.

We shy away from love because we're afraid of the pain that comes with loving. The cure for this fear, paradoxically, is to love more. When my son hugged me, it triggered a mysterious and painful anger that awakened me to my subconscious fears. Once alerted, I chose to be more loving and accept my vulnerability. It was either that or stay angry and keep some distance from my son. To walk the tightrope of life with grace, we must continually choose to love despite the ever dangerous forces of fear and unconsciousness that can trip us up faster than a horse can swish its tail.

After observing the process of grief and renewal with thousands of dying patients, the renowned psychiatrist Dr. Elisabeth Kubler-Ross noted that the thoughts of people approaching death turn almost exclusively to intimate relationships. Only the love that people have shared throughout their lives remains of comfort and value to them.

If living with love and intimate relationships is such a basic need and so pervasive a force, why are we so poor at it? Why are there so many wars, so many problems? Why do sincere, good people, people who desperately want their lives to work, who want to find joy, companionship, and cooperation, so often come up empty handed? It is not unusual for a parent, initially ripe with love and devotion for his or her small child, to be mired in a generational conflict fifteen or twenty years later—the child rejecting the parents' values and claiming that any love shown was impure. And how many marriages start so brightly, full of faithful promises and joyous expectations, only to crash into bitter, ugly disputes full of betrayal, accusation, and blame? Something is wrong. Something is missing. Somehow our fear of love and our inability to risk wisely destroys the love we seek.

One premise of this book is that we are out of balance or alignment with an integral component of life—risk. Instead of using risk to empower our lives—accepting and working with the uncertainty inherent in existence—we let our fears confuse and overwhelm us.

Risk is part of life. It can't be avoided. Helen Keller wrote:

Security is mostly a superstition. It does not exist in nature nor do children as a whole experience it. Avoiding danger is no safer in the long run than outright exposure. Life is either a daring adventure or nothing.

When we push risk away it boomerangs back and hits us from behind. Risk wakes us up. We need it to create passion. But using it well is not so easy.

Ellen is a good example. She began therapy after realizing she had to choose between her husband of twenty years or a different man she was falling in love with. Outwardly Ellen's life was the picture of respectability—a two-professional, three-child family, happily ensconced in the suburbs. But she admitted: "I never heard my parents fight. I was brought up country-club conservative, and I fit the part except that I drink and drive, have mad, illicit affairs, and live on an unhealthy edge."

Ellen was bored and needed excitement to know that her brief time on this planet mattered. Because her early life had been so proper and staid, she craved emotional intensity. As a child anger was forbidden and exuberance discouraged. She received no training in how to manage her natural and healthy desire to risk. So she created a secret wild side that she is both ashamed and proud of. To save her marriage she must reveal this hidden self to her husband—because he doesn't know who she is. This is a risk of terrifying proportions, but perhaps the only one that can save her relationship.

Many clients have confessed that as they near the object of their intense desire, be it a romantic relationship or job improvement, they get scared and begin to sabotage themselves. They let their fear of risk overwhelm them, so they are stopped short of reaching their goals. One client who was physically abused as a child, for example, loves children and craves the closeness of a family; but he simply cannot trust himself to not harm a future child. So when a woman gets too close to him he pushes her away. His life revolves around a tragic cycle of seeking love only to pull back into isolation and loneliness whenever love draws close.

We're afraid to love. Loving well requires us to live boldly in the face of the risk that life is. Many of us forget that we do have the power to choose to not let our fears of intimacy or success overpower us. Too often we don't know how to make that choice.

We crave intimacy but find it incredibly difficult to create; one step forward, one step back. There are few successful role models. The information that helps us move towards living a passionate and deeply loving life is difficult to decipher, and even harder to practice. The craving for intimacy amidst a tug of war between our love and fear is a primary struggle for many.

One client confessed that she couldn't imagine surviving the possible death of a child of her own. So unspeakable was that fear and pain that she preferred instead the safety of an empty womb. The risk of unbearable loss simply seemed too great.

To love well is difficult; it is also scary. Life is no fairy tale. Mice are mice, not coachmen; and pumpkins are pumpkins, not carriages. It's great that the Prince fell in love with Cinderella's tiny feet and that they lived happily ever after. But for the rest of us, the only magic wand is the one that we ourselves pick up on the day we firmly commit to become a better human being.

The Purpose of This Book

Laura had been trained from an early age to stifle her sensitivity and self-expression. Her parents wanted her to be "tough." So they nailed her every time she displayed vulnerability. She kept hoping, often desperately, that they would start being supportive and kind. They never did.

Thirty years later, Laura was fighting to stave off divorce. She had withdrawn from her husband because the risks associated with loving him no longer made sense. She was weary from fighting with a guy who put her down just as her parents had.

She knew that to give her marriage another chance she would have to let herself be vulnerable and accept that her husband was also scared and trying to change. But after fifteen years of marriage she no longer believed things could be different. Better, she reasoned, to take her kids and strike out on her own— as hard as that might be—than to relive her childhood trauma of desperately hoping that her parents would change.

This couple's issues were not as complex as Laura claimed. They didn't fight about money, the kids, or the way responsibilities were divided. They fought about fighting. Civility and kindness had gone into hibernation as a deep angry freeze settled in through the years. They needed guidelines for better communication and perspective about their lives.

But Laura was gun shy. She was four-fifths out the door when the counseling began and unwilling to make much effort. Within several weeks she recognized the withdrawal pattern from her childhood. No one had ever been there for her. "I lived with high expectations, but no guidance," she told me.

"What a devastating combination. This time it will be different," I reassured her. "I'll be on your side. You'll get the information you need to fight fair and you'll have my caring and support." I explained that I would make it safer for her to be vulnerable and help her husband understand how to do the same. "You aren't a kid anymore," I told her. "You have resources now you didn't have then. Stick around, you won't regret it."

She knew that if she walked she was leaving more than her husband; she also would be leaving the hope that her childhood traumas could be healed. Although she needed coaxing, she did stick around and accepted that a good marriage requires hard work and a willingness to risk. Her husband was not oblivious and also worked hard. Together they saved their relationship.

This book is being written so that if, like Laura, you're facing a challenge in your life, you can get some encouragement, inspiration, and guidance to stick around and work on it. Spiritual and psychological growth takes courage. I hope to inspire you with stories of people who have blazed some trails and shown us with their actions that loving and risking are worth it. The stories come from my life as a father, a husband, and a professional therapist.

Unlike the realm of professional sports, where television crews cover virtually every muscle twitch, the telling moments in our lives usually occur in private. As a therapist I have had the privileged opportunity of listening to thousands of people intimately describe their risks, their fears, and their secret aspirations.

These pages invite you to immerse yourself in people's lives as they stand poised or trembling on the tightrope that life often is. In any risky endeavor the pleasures of accomplishment are heightened by the perils we face. We'll look closely at different crossroads people meet as they try to determine which path is best. Some stories describe minor choices or issues—problems that arise daily in the course of every life. Others focus on crucial turning points of obvious importance. Each story is designed to move you a little closer towards your own power and magnificence so like the artist on the high wire, you can balance your life with equanimity and ease.

The book is organized around five core values that, taken together, provide perspective and a set of tools to help us embrace the mystery of life. They are honesty, respect, responsibility, commitment, and balance. The glue holding these together is our intention. For clarity's sake, I discuss them separately; but as life unfolds, such distinctions break down. Mastery arises when these core values operate in harmony.

A Zen master once described enlightenment as the acceptance of reality exactly as it is, moment to moment. I don't know about enlightenment, but I do know that not accepting life as it is produces suffering. We live with risk. Trying to make life safe when that is not its nature is a foolish and impossible goal. Peace arises with the acceptance of life and ourselves as we are. Becoming adept at working with these five core values provides us with a foundation from which growth and expansion naturally proceed.

The theme of accepting reality is central to working effectively with risk. To accept reality as it is requires vigilance. Our resistance to or non-acceptance of life is so ordinary we don't even see it. I pull up to a supermarket line and notice after a while, for example, that it is moving slowly because the clerk is a trainee. There are now people behind me, so I'm sandwiched in. Do I relax and see this as an opportunity to enjoy a moment with nothing going on? Or do I tense up and impatiently wonder whether I'll have enough time for something else?

In this culture we're conditioned to hurry. A hundred times a day—or is it a thousand?—our minds rebel against reality, wishing it to be different. An undercurrent of complaining runs through most of our lives. Yet if I were dying of cancer or recovering from a stroke, I'd want nothing more than to be physically capable of still caring for myself, of going shopping, of waiting in line.

Some of this book provides specific communication tools and information that can help sort out the complexity of life. We need to ask the right questions and think productively about the issues that are germane to *our* life. We need to know that the battles we're fighting are the right ones. This requires a thorough grounding in those basic communication tools that help us confront our issues effectively. Just as a master carpenter is helpless without the appropriate tools, we need to understand how to communicate well to move safely from one risky moment to the next.

As a therapist, I watch in amazement and horror as loving people with poor communication skills destroy their family. Sometimes the remedy is as simple as reminding people not to interrupt. It wouldn't surprise me if fifty percent of all marital issues can be traced to this easily ameliorated problem. That's an amazing statement, not an exaggeration. Basic communication skills can make the difference between success and failure in love.

Much of what I write about, you may already know. But this book can serve as a powerful reminder to return to the basics. One example of a great communication tool is described in Aldous Huxley's book *Island*, which describes his version of Utopia. This ideal land was filled with talking parrots; each one knew only one word and said it often. The word was "Attention," and it served to remind the islanders to be fully aware at each moment.

Sometimes, however, I'll be painting broader strokes that offer inspiration and perspective on life and our general struggles. I move around from the personal to the universal and from the general to the specific. I find this style helps clients integrate information more easily.

One teacher said, "Run from anyone who tells you that life is not difficult." Making tough changes and accepting ourselves as we are is not easy. There are times when grace is obvious, but more often we're lost in shadows or darkness. I write to offer encouragement and perspective, as well as humor and pathos. To accept the thousands of joys and sorrows that life in all its devastating richness brings—this takes courage and skill.

1

Insight and Action

A FLASH of rage careened through my body when I saw my seven-year-old riding his two-wheeler in a dangerous spot. My only request had been that he stay away from that corner where cars turn into our road. Twice in the past few days I had controlled my anger and had gently but firmly reminded him of this. Declaring ten percent of the street off-limits seemed like a modest imposition on his freedom.

This time I had had it. Lunging for the door, I burst outside. Fire burned in my chest as I ran toward him. Riding a bicycle dangerously was unacceptable. A *much stronger* communication was about to explode.

Just as I came within his earshot and was about to let out a full-bodied yell, I stopped cold: A memory pierced my consciousness. Retracing my steps, I sat on the ground and leaned against my door. I was stunned. A story a client had recently told me about his father's verbal lacerations echoed in my head: "When my father yelled at me, I would see his mouth moving but I didn't hear his words. Everything slowed down, and I'd get a kind of blank, queasy feeling."

His story, I knew, was a common one. Children frequently cope with perceived aggression by blocking out much of the experience. Through the years many clients had shared similar stories. The realization that my own child would likely view his father from the same silent, terrified vantage point stopped me.

I needed my son to absorb this crucial communication about safety. Leaning wearily now against my door, I let myself experience the wave of angry feelings still surging within me. Standing quietly for a minute, I realized that my rage stemmed from the utter lack of control that I faced as a parent. Ultimately, I could never erase the possibility that my son might be killed violently in a horrific accident. My helplessness shook me to the core.

Just as I advise my clients to consider worst-case scenarios when contemplating risks, I began to explicitly visualize my nightmare. I imagined running out of the house moments after my child had been run over and picking him up as he lay in a pool of blood. The idea of losing my vital, exuberant son left me sobbing.

I wasn't really angry, I was scared of losing him—scared of my potential grief. After gaining some control, I picked myself up and, tears still trickling down my face, walked toward my boy and tenderly called to him, "Come sit down with me, I need to talk to you."

Hilly was confused by my tears. I sat him on my lap and then shared my experience. My voice was quiet and soothing. "You were riding your bike in a dangerous place and that really scared me. I don't think you appreciate how much responsibility is required now that you can ride a bike. I can't imagine anything more horrible than losing you in a foolish bike accident." I paused a while to let my words sink in. My son nestled against me. "Do you know what it means to me to have you in my life?" I said, my tears flowing freely. "You're everything to me, you light up my life. I love being your daddy, watching you grow up. Life without you would feel horrible."

Moved by my obvious love, my boy hugged me tightly. When our embrace was over I said, "Please drive your bike safely. It's not all right to ride so close to the corner. The cars may not see you in time." Looking into each other's eyes, we soaked up the intimacy of the moment.

"I promise daddy," he said. "I won't drive where you think it's unsafe." His bike riding indiscretion wasn't repeated.

Later, I pondered the event. Everything could have turned out so differently. I felt blessed. I was on the verge of dishing out some punishment—taking his bike away or grounding him, or both. In retrospect I knew that either of those angry reactions would have had a deleterious effect on my goal of simply making my child as safety-conscious as possible. Worse still, I knew that an angry parent often unwittingly sets up a psychological rebellion in a child that practically forces a kid to act foolishly. Helping a child maintain the delicate balance between a healthy, adventurous spirit and an intelligent sense of caution is no easy task. Blasting a kid with uncontrolled fury does not accomplish that balance. No wonder I felt good afterward: This time I had been successful.

Insight and Action—Two Components of Growth

Life happens fast. Too fast. Something wonderful happens and we don't know why or how to create it again. Something horrible happens and we don't learn its lesson well enough to not repeat the painful patterns over and over. Turning the energy and intensity of rage into loving and effective communication is not common. This chapter outlines basic steps that allow that to happen.

Two telling moments made a difference during my experience with my son. The first was when I saw that my anger was not going to help the situation. The second was when I acted expressively and appropriately based on that insight. That took courage.

Insight combined with appropriate action were the two components intrinsic to the heartwarming experience I had with my son. I believe that all growth results from this two-step process— insight plus appropriate action.

Insight may be nothing other than profound common sense

or wisdom. When we have insight we can think clearly in the presence of our pain. But thinking clearly is not enough. Insight alone doesn't create the desired results. There are brilliant and insightful people whose understanding and knowledge are vast, but whose lives are unhappy—even tragic—because they don't have the courage to act appropriately with their insight. Without that courage, insight fuels despair and frustration.

Joan was thirteen. Her mother was having yet another temper tantrum, screaming in her daughter's face and viciously slapping her.

"Then the eeriest thing happened," Joan recounted years later. "I will always remember it. Right in the middle of her hysteria, as she's screaming and hitting me, and as I'm crying myself—freaked out by her assault—she stopped. For just a moment she looked at me differently, and told me that she wished I could stop her when she got like this. The moment of sanity passed and she then continued her attack."

"So she knew that she was out of control and that she was being a monster?"

"Yes," Joan sighed. "But she didn't have the courage to stop. I guess she was letting me know that she knew she was crazy."

Joan's mother lacked courage. She had a fleeting insight but, alone, it wasn't enough to help either herself or her daughter.

Our culture's notion of courage is a little warped. We customarily think of courage in heroic terms—like someone risking their life for another. Opportunities for a physical demonstration of such courage are rare.

For Joan's mother to be courageous, she would have had to admit that she needed help. She also would have had to apologize to her daughter, and then stop the destructive patterns that had been terrorizing her child for years. My action with my son was courageous because I admitted that he had power over me. When we admit our weaknesses and vulnerabilities we are exercising courage, so long as that admission carries with it a commitment to change destructive behavior.

To act courageously requires that we give up some part of ourselves. I had to give up my anger and any illusion of safety. Joan's mom would have had to give up her sense of control. The risk we face when we give up these things feels palpable at the time. Kahlil Gibran writes in *The Prophet*:

All you have shall some day be given;
Therefore give now, that the season of giving may be
yours and not your inheritors'.

Courage can manifest differently for men and women. Men tend to be more comfortable with anger and so block the vulnerability inherent in expressing tenderness and sadness. Historically, boys were trained to be tough. Until recently most men were expected to fight and, if necessary, die for their homeland. This created a tendency to suppress the softer elements of human character. But a mystique that links courage to being assertive and powerful no longer serves us or accurately reflects true courage.

Many women, on the other hand, are more comfortable with sadness, and often block the primacy of their anger and sexuality. Aggressive women threaten many men. It's not unusual to label a women a bitch for simply being an assertive, unsentimental businesswoman. As a result, when women feel angry they often are more comfortable displaying sadness or vulnerability—thus mislabeling their experience as sadness. That is why they are often angry at themselves afterwards for crying or showing emotion.

It takes courage to assert ourselves. What's important to remember is that acting courageously does not mean acting heroically. It may mean seizing a moment and admitting a weakness or manifesting a strength.

Courage and insight feed each other. The best way to deepen our insight is to act courageously: With each courageous act, more insights arise. As this spiral is honored and nurtured, our wisdom and happiness slowly deepen. The motivation for more courageous action also deepens.

Separating Thoughts and Feelings—Susan

The entry into this cycle of growth is insight. We can't act courageously until we know how to think clearly. Thinking with clarity requires making crucial distinctions. There is a difference, for example, between our thoughts and our feelings. Without an increasing clarity about that distinction, and other distinctions, the insight process cannot unfurl. So we start here.

Susan didn't know who she was, but at the beginning of therapy she did not realize that. She was too busy not being like her mother to find out how she felt.

If she was uncomfortable during her first session, she hid it behind her exuberance and charm. Her speech was as fluent and bold as her bright colored blouse and the flaming yellow ribbons in her wavy long brown hair. "I hate rules," she said, eyes dancing. "My creative spirit thrives on spontaneity and chaos." She continued, "I'm not sure you can help me. I've been to other therapists and they want me to grow up. I heard that you encourage people to work with their self-expression, so I thought I'd give you a try."

"What's wrong with being a grown-up? Grown-ups get to choose where they want to go, have sex lives, and make money."

"I like all those things. But as an artist, I don't want to be bound by society's rigid rules."

"Do you think happy, spontaneous kids don't like boundaries or rules?"

"Rules and happiness don't belong in the same sentence," she shot back passionately.

"So if I keep my agreements and pay my taxes, that means I can't also be happy?"

"You're confusing me."

"You sound confused, Susan, and I suspect that's why you're

here. But I'm not confusing you. I'm only asking questions to help you figure out how you think."

"Artists shouldn't need to think. We feel, we intuit, we create."

"Artists especially need to think. Susan, why are you here?"

She wasn't really sure, but in the next few months her story unfolded.

Although she was a talented artist, her business was falling apart. She didn't honor deadlines, forgot appointments, and owed money. The problem traced back to her strict religious mother, who declared war on Susan's daring sensual spirit by demanding conformity and respectability. Rules became synonymous for Susan with rigidity, lifelessness, and boredom. "My mother was more concerned about order than about helping me explore my universe. She hated my creativity and flair, and she discouraged me from becoming an artist. I felt like I was in a straitjacket."

The more I heard, the more abusive her past sounded. "When I was twelve," Susan continued, "she took away my art supplies and forbade me to draw after I drew some mildly erotic sketches—kids' stuff really." Tears of rage and grief streamed down her face as she recalled the memory. "Childhood was like basic training. As a kid I vowed I would be different."

As she vented her feelings, exploring her past, she recognized the extent to which her attitudes were rooted in her upbringing. She began to trust that I had her best interest in mind, but she still held back. She resisted making changes in her life. She had so identified herself as a rebel that any conformity—even conformity to the therapy process—felt like spiritual death.

"Every time I make a commitment," she snapped, "even if it's to a customer, I get this gnawing feeling inside like people are closing in on me and I shut down. I don't want to give up my power. I don't want to answer to anyone. Maybe it's childish, but I don't care."

"You do care, Susan," I shot back. "That's why you came

here. The way you think is killing you." My voice carried a gentle passion. "You need to separate the *concept* of rules, how you think about them, from your *feelings* of oppression. That pain you feel in your guts when you make a commitment is coming from something in your past. It's not coming from what you're doing today. You're not seeing the big picture and you're lying to yourself. You're lying because you're afraid to risk a new way of thinking about yourself and about self-discipline."

"Self-discipline," she retorted. "Yuk! You sound like my mother!"

"I may *sound* like her, but I'm *not* your mother nor your enemy. Your mom thought your feelings were her enemy so she stifled them. But you've made them your enemy too, because you hide behind them even when they are obviously unbalanced. Do you understand?"

Susan looked shaken. She was trying to let it in.

"So I'm hurting myself when I say that I can do whatever I *feel* like doing?"

"Exactly. To keep your artistic spirit alive as a child you defended it by rebelling and developed it as a way to think about *all* of life. But with time comes changes. These thought-patterns are outdated. You have options today that you never had as a child. That's the good news. The bad news is that you haven't been seeing that."

We become slaves to our outdated ideas when we take them as universal truths. Like Susan we must make sure that what we believe helps us move in the direction we want, and that we're not lying to ourselves to avoid difficult realities. The intensity of Susan's stifled childhood feelings cast a dark shadow over everything. She saw society and all rules as the enemy in the same way that she once viewed her mother.

Our thoughts and values today often reflect the way we were taught to live as kids. If our parents had deep-seated prejudices, we are likely to carry them on unconsciously. If we hate or distrust the way our parents thought, we sometimes go to the opposite extreme and adopt values and thought-patterns that are diametrically opposite those we were raised with. But then we're still not thinking for ourselves, because we depend upon our parents for our reference point. In either case, their prejudices (strong thoughts attached to angry feelings) restrict our freedom.

Susan realized that her own thought processes were as rigid and as unhelpful to her as an adult as her mom's were to her as a child. In seeking to avoid being like her mother, she had turned into someone quite similar. Susan began to realize that "rules" themselves are not the problem—her mother's rigid way of administering them was.

As Susan's insight into her own muddled thinking deepened, she brought major changes into her life. She paid her bills and kept her appointments, but it wasn't easy. Old habits die hard and, new insights notwithstanding, she often failed to act courageously.

"How was your week?" I asked as she settled warily onto the sofa in my office one afternoon.

"Not too good, Mitch, if you have to know." She smiled. I smiled back. "I'm sorry you're having such a tough time. What happened?"

"Old stuff. I blew off an important work commitment. At least I caught myself doing it."

"Insight takes us half-way."

"Yeah, I know," she mocked me. "Insight *plus* action." As the story unfurled, it became obvious that Susan needed to apologize to a customer who, by now, would be irate.

"I don't think she's going to accept my apology. How many times can you screw up and still get away with it?"

"I guess she thinks your apologies are pretty worthless. Is there any way to bring more sincerity to this process?"

"I could offer my services at a reduced rate—to compensate

for all her trouble, I guess." I sat silently and watched as her face took on the expression of a stubborn little girl. After a long pause she continued angrily. "No way. That would make me feel incredibly uncomfortable and beholden to her. Besides I need the money. I'm not working for nothing."

After a long pause, I said, "There's a part of you that finds it so hard to change—even though you know it only makes your life harder." I spoke with great tenderness because I saw how deeply she was struggling to act courageously. My heart went out to her. "I wish you weren't so hard on yourself."

She seemed surprised—shocked even—by my tone. "I thought for sure you were going to tell me how bad I am. Boy, I really have some wires crossed." Then, after a long pause, she added, "By next week I will have cleaned this mess up. I'm not just going to reduce my rate, I'm going to give her my services for free. She deserves it."

Did my kindness help Susan act courageously? Maybe.

When we realize that our actions aren't aligned with our insights, it's often helpful to bring some compassion to ourselves. Talking to others about our travails makes it easier to act courageously. We can see what we need to do and get some support.

Susan could act with courage because she separated her thoughts from her feelings. She felt rebellious but she didn't completely identify with that feeling as she had in the past. Her mom had infuriated her by mocking her—calling her "God's stubborn little girl." With me she also felt stubborn, but her actions reflected her commitment to her growth.

How we feel and how we think are distinct. Like Susan, most of us confuse the two. Such distinctions weren't available to us as kids, when all sensations and experiences were lumped together. But as we get older we can start to see how our emotional pain blocks our ability to think critically. Mary Poppins once said, "Practically perfect people never permit sentiment to muddle their thinking." Those of us less highly evolved have to be diligent to not let our uncomfortable feelings of anger, pain, sorrow, frustration, and fear muddle our clarity.

Separating our thoughts from our feelings is essential to gain insight into why we act as we do. Sometimes it can mean the difference between life and death. When Janice lost her husband after forty years of marriage, for example, she was heartbroken. Elderly people often give up their will to live when a long-term partner dies. Janice was tempted to make her grief at her husband's passing mean that life was no longer worth living. If she attached that thought to her grief she would have slipped into a serious depression. By realizing that thoughts and feelings are distinct, she was able to feel her sadness but not adopt a negative attitude toward life. Of course, there was struggle. She had to adopt different support systems. She had to rely more heavily on her children—something she hated to do. She had to create a different life. By staying alert to this crucial separation between thoughts and feelings, we increase our capacity for insight while paving the way for courageous action.

Separating Feelings—Anger and Sadness

In addition to the insight that comes from separating thoughts and feelings, there is another important distinction to make—this time between our different feelings.

Let's go back to the story of Hilly and the bike. In the course of a few moments I experienced a wide range of feelings—anger, sadness, fear, horror, confusion, joy, and intimacy. At first I was angry, livid, fuming. After some confusion, the experience gave way to horror and ultimately grief. Looking back, it's easy to conclude that my anger then was a substitute for grief that I was afraid to feel. I believe this is also true of most anger in general. Anger pushes away the unwanted feeling.

Most of the time anger is not a primary or core feeling. We get angry because it's less painful to be angry than to be hurt. Hurt is humiliating, hurt is powerless, hurt leaves us at the mercy of the universe. Anger makes us feel like we can right a wrong, make a difference, be in control. But anger often backfires. If I had acted without being conscious of my underlying grief, and screamed at Hilly for riding his bike unsafely, I would have forgotten the incident quickly. Hilly would have filed his experience into the category called "scary, out of control adult—try to avoid." It would not have been a successful communication because it would not have made my son a safer bike rider.

My unwillingness to face the primacy of my grief would have resulted ultimately in a damaging communication to my son. When our communications don't achieve their desired goals, it's smart to suspect that we're being less than fully authentic—and that a riskier, more honest communication is needed. This is where the maxim, "The truth will set you free" has power. A basic rule of thumb: If you're not getting what you want, you're not using your feelings in a way that helps you.

In the past fifteen years, I have developed a way of working with intense emotions that allows me to help my clients fully express their feelings. I approach painful or negative feelings through two categories—anger and sadness. In the bike story, my anger was masking my sadness. Although this is commonly the case, there are times when anger is a primary feeling which, communicated effectively, can help us meet our needs. Just as all the colors in the rainbow can be reduced into red, yellow, and green, the three primary colors, so painful feelings are usually, at their core, either sadness or anger.

It is common to feel lousy or anxious or depressed, and to not know how to express or release that feeling. When I feel that way, or one of my family members or clients reports this kind of distress, I invariably ask, "Are you angry or sad?" The question usually elicits a strong reaction that makes it easier to know what's upsetting them. Try it. When you're feeling out of sorts, check to see whether you're angry or sad. It's my experience that at the core of nearly all upsets is some unexpressed anger or sadness.

Discovering whether anger or sadness is the primary emotion takes a willingness to listen deeply and respectfully to ourselves. Some real-life stories in the next few pages will help sort feelings into their primary and secondary components to help us gain insight into why some communications backfire.

Primary Sadness

Alice and Paul had been fighting for years before they came for marital therapy. He was angry, she was bitter. Each had an armload of reasons why the other was ruining their life. They fought about money, sex, the children. Paul was often angry with his wife and she would lash back at him. Meaningful dialogue had ceased long ago.

Each communicated from their secondary feeling, which in this case was anger. As their referee I insisted on certain ground rules, the first of which was no interrupting. For many weeks their fighting continued.

Over time, they began to see a similarity in their pain. They were both hurting, both lonely, both feeling betrayed. As they got the hang of respectful listening, each heard the other's pain as pain and not as condemnation. Because each allowed the other's anger to be heard, an undercurrent of resentment no longer pervaded everything. Increasingly, the couple realized how much sadness and loneliness each of them experienced. A genuine compassion arose that began melting their differences.

Most of our daily, petty frustrations, our annoyances with others or ourselves, are secondary feelings of tension covering up a basic dissatisfaction with or grief for our life. This is, of course, hard to let in. It's much more comfortable to be pissed off at your co-worker, or the lousy driver who switches lanes without signaling, than to start examining the primacy of unexpressed and unprocessed grief. I caught myself before blasting my kid because I knew the stakes were high, and because I had only recently heard a client describe his inability to absorb angry retorts.

Many times we are ineffectively angry. There's no need to

scream at a kid to pick up her toys, for example, if she only needs a stern reminder. A communication doesn't have to be emotional to be strong. Firmness is neither anger nor sadness, it is just firmness. To be respected, firmness needs to be communicated with clarity and power, but not excessive emotion. Dog training manuals remind owners that emotionality only confuses the animal; it also confuses kids and most of the rest of us.

The best trick I know to stop indulging in petty arguments and defensive wrangles, which seldom express primary feelings, is to listen respectfully. One time when Lindy (my ex-wife) was angry with me I remembered my advice (insight) and, instead of defending myself, practiced (action) silent non-resistance. As my temptation to "explain" my side of the story grew stronger, I suspected that I must be off somehow—why else would I have such a strong reaction? "Just listen and keep your mouth shut," I begged myself. As I stood only a foot away from her, feeling blasted, I noticed a tightening in my stomach. Surprised by this reaction, I paid closer attention. I had lots of stomach aches as a kid. Was I reliving some childhood memory? A vague memory of fighting with my mother surfaced. Then I looked back at Lindy and actually *heard* what she wanted—an apology from me about something I had done earlier. I saw my choice. I could give her the benefit of the doubt, apologize, and have a peaceful evening—or fight it out. It was a no-brainer once I saw to the heart of the matter.

By acting wisely (in this case, simply standing quietly), I felt my anger as a pain in my stomach and broke the cycle. The experience of the feeling was pure; it completed itself, bringing with it an insight. When we experience our feelings purely and fully, we can release them. The more fully we can appropriately express our grief the more quickly it will pass and provide us with insight and wisdom.

Full Expression

To feel our sadness requires that we not shy away from the risks inherent in life. We must accept those risks and the pain inherent in life if we want to love deeply. The story of Hilly jumping into my arms saying "I love you" illustrates this. But the ramifications go deeper. In writing about love, Gibran reminds us that if we are only seeking love's peace or pleasure and are not willing to experience the risk and pain of love:

> *Then it is better for you that you cover your nakedness and*
> *pass out of love's threshing floor,*
> *Into the seasonless world where you shall laugh, but not*
> *all your laughter, and weep, but not all your tears.*

If we want all our laughter, if we want to live fully, we must also experience all our tears. We must express ourselves fully. Without such full expression, we won't earn insights and so we'll be afraid to act decisively.

Several days after Lindy told me she wanted to divorce, my grief reached its absolute zenith. I was sitting on my bed, quite alone, sobbing. All day at work I had stifled back my tears, knowing I had to wait for a more appropriate time to cry. Finally, at the end of the day, alone, I abandoned myself to the pain. As my anguish intensified, each heaving breath brought burning pain to my abdomen. Nothing was more important than having that relationship succeed. My feelings of failure were almost unbearable.

After I had been sobbing for I don't know how long, feeling profound despair, I heard a single word clearly enunciated: "Enough." I was taken aback by this message from within. Like a hydrant suddenly shut down, my tears stopped. I became quiet and still. Some part of my inner being recognized that I could no longer sustain the intensity of my pain and loss. I had suffered enough. A wave of relief and well-being replaced the grief. I was all right. My loss, I knew, would arise again and again. But for now, it had completed itself. I had "cried all my tears" and it was time to ease off.

The experience left me surprisingly confident and energized. There is a time and place for everything. I knew at that moment that if I cried any more I would be indulging in my grief, over-dramatizing it somehow, allowing it to manipulate me. I also knew that if I had cried any less I would have been holding back and not fully and adequately expressing my pain. I wanted to be neither a drama king holding a pity party nor a tight-lipped con-stipated macho guy staving off his feelings under the guise of toughing life out. For that moment I had reached a perfect bal-ance. By giving myself to the grief instead of resisting it, I let it complete itself and educate me. Now I know when I sit with someone in pain that it is futile to try to control the experience. The pain must be respected and allowed full expression.

Letting myself feel the totality of my experience or counsel-ing another to do the same can be dangerous. It requires some guidelines. Letting ourselves go means trusting that our emotions are our allies and won't be destructively out of balance, irre-sponsible, or disrespectful. But that was exactly how we experienced most painful emotionality as children, so we don't trust ourselves to feel fully.

The ground rule for self-expression is simple: The intent must not be to cause harm to myself or another nor can there be any intention to manipulate others in an unhealthy way to satisfy my personal needs. In short, I must express myself honestly, respon-sibly, and respectfully. Obviously a high level of self-discipline and self-awareness must be present before we do this cleanly and effectively. This is why so many of us retreat into the seasonless world where we laugh but not all our laughter, and weep but not all our tears.

The more we are willing to express our feelings fully, the

more we'll be apt to seize those risky opportunities that allow us to act decisively from our insights.

Primary Anger

Generally speaking, anger is a smokescreen or mask for grief. But just as there are exceptions in the rules of grammar, so there are crucial exceptions here also. Anger is sometimes a primary feeling, the expression of which is appropriate. Anger has been bred into us as part of nature's survival strategy. Without it and the willingness to defend ourselves, we would be dominated by others. Our anger becomes triggered when survival issues arise. This explains one part of my reaction to my son's bike riding escapade. It also explains why, in the privacy of an automobile, an extraordinary amount of hostile feeling comes up whenever our sense of safety is threatened.

Anger is complex. Sometimes it is not in our best interest to express our anger and we're better off to keep still and save its expression for a different time. Sometimes we must express our anger spontaneously and loudly. Sometimes we must be cold and calculated.

Since anger is a passion that can be highly damaging if unattended and unstructured, we have to make sure we're thinking about it intelligently and honestly. The ground rules for the expression of anger are similar to those listed earlier for all self-expression. Our intent must not be to cause harm to another—but wait. This type of pacifism would leave me or my loved ones unfairly vulnerable to an attack! If someone is harming my child, for example, I would stop them by trusting myself to let my anger unleash itself in the form needed to accomplish that goal. So the ground rule carries a modifier: If someone is causing unjustifiable injury, it then becomes appropriate to prevent that violation, channeling anger with control and flexibility as necessary.

Unless we have been wisely trained in the appropriate

expression of anger, though, it's hard to channel our rage successfully. Mostly we learn the hard way, from trial and error. A good deal of therapy consists of helping clients recognize when anger is appropriate and finding successful ways to share it and vent it.

My office is sound-proofed for that reason, and also comes equipped with a punching bag. The last time I used the thick red radiator hose to pummel the bag and vent my frustration offers an example of productively channeling anger.

I began my career in a community-based mental health program. After several years of valuable experience, I took the risk of starting a private practice. In those first few months I was hungry for referrals.

One day a physician called to set up an introductory session. I was walking on air, already counting the numerous referrals I thought he'd generate. Unfortunately, I forgot to check my appointment book on the morning of our first meeting. No one was at my office to answer his loud, repeated knocks.

When I realized what had happened, I was not only horrified by my sloppiness but fearful that I was subconsciously sabotaging myself and my career. I also knew that I would have to face one of my best friends, who was the source of the referral.

For about fifteen minutes I smashed the bag and yelled, over and over with each blow, "Check your appointment book each morning." I didn't denigrate myself as I knew that might only increase future unconsciousness: I was entitled to the mistake as long as it wasn't repeated. So I pounded a single message into my brain, channeling all my rage and horror into a commitment to check my book each day. My rage wasn't blocking any grief, it was pure and simple anger at myself for being unconscious. I caused no harm to myself or to another as I released my rage. Also I was not just "blowing off steam": I was putting the energy of the anger into the commitment to check the book. Soon I was able to forgive myself. I graciously apologized to the physician and to my friend and was able to not beat up on myself.

It's risky to let anger out. One stiff-lipped client told me, "I am so angry that if I ever start hitting that punching bag I'm afraid I would never stop." But when we express our feelings powerfully and appropriately, a healing energy surfaces.

When Robert was a teenager, for example, he was attacked in an alley. His adrenaline and fighting skills kicked in. When he darted off a few moments later, his attacker was bleeding and badly wounded on the ground. The fight, and his successful self-defense, left Robert afraid of his own capacity for violence. He consciously sought to repress all his angry feelings.

Years later, he found it difficult to fight constructively with his wife and to effectively discipline his kids. Describing the incident in the alley terrified him, because he didn't want to experience those feelings again.

Gradually, over weeks, he relived the trauma and was able to vent his rage with increasing levels of passion. The sessions served to debrief him and allow him to find a new balance in his emotional life. By risking an appropriate expression of anger, working with it as a primary feeling, he successfully reclaimed the part of himself that he left behind as a teenager. Before he could feel remorse for the event and make peace with his past actions, he first had to vent his rage.

Sometimes it's difficult to discern whether anger or sadness is our primary emotion. If we give ourselves to an experience, listening well and knowing that our intent is not to harm, we'll soon discover which feeling is more authentic or primary.

Pam, a mother brought up in a strict religious household, believed that expressing any anger was a sign of poor character. When her six-year-old son annoyed her, she thought something was wrong with her for feeling aggravated. The boy sensed his mother's fear and powerlessness and pressed his advantage. Instead of getting angry with her son and setting reasonable limits, Pam became frustrated with herself. Occasionally she would lose it, screaming hysterically. Then she'd apologize and feel guilty. She was more comfortable blaming herself and feeling bad than trusting herself to feel her anger and use that feeling to discipline her son effectively.

If what we're doing isn't working, we're misreading our feelings. Once I validated Pam's anger and told her it was perfectly normal for a mother to get angry with a child, she tuned in to herself and started discovering how to use her anger to set appropriate boundaries.

Tension is often a precursor of anger. If we can get to it before it builds and attend to it properly, we can use it to energize ourselves.

Because of a transportation problem, my oldest son, Peter, once returned home from a summer trip to Europe only sixteen hours before he was scheduled to be back in college. As he unpacked and then packed again, I could see him struggling with the abrupt transition. Next thing I knew, Pete was down in my office (in the ground floor of our home), pounding the punching bag. Through the soundproofing we heard a muffled din. When he appeared again twenty minutes later, a broad grin on his face, he let us know, "Now I feel ready to go back to school." Pete wasn't so much angry as out of sorts and unfocused. He used his energy to invigorate himself and focus on a goal, which in this case was functioning well at school. Because he wasn't afraid of his anger, he could use it to help mobilize himself for action.

There are many other appropriate times to be angry. Just as I was angry at myself for blowing that appointment, I express my anger when others break their agreements with me. Of paramount importance is that my expression be designed not to exact punishment but to correct a mistake.

When I'm angry with my children or my wife Kathy, our interactions follow a pattern. After I express myself, one of three things occurs. Sometimes, I get an apology. The problem is then over. Sometimes, I get an angry retort back. Then I've got to listen respectfully to the other person's experience. Since my anger is often a sign that I am missing something or being dishonest with myself, the listening serves as a check. Often I see my error and apologize.

As unpleasant as anger is, we can't get to the heart of the matter until we've had a chance to air our grievances. Ninety percent of all disagreements in our family are resolved in the first two categories. Now and then a longer, more complex discussion is necessary to sort the issues relating to the source of the frustration.

The two primary feelings of anger and sadness don't always fit neatly into discernible containers. Robert's rage at his attacker in the alley may have kept him alive. When he allowed himself to dwell on it, it was at first a primary feeling. Over time, as it was fully expressed, it evolved into grief. Robert had lost a part of himself for many years and he needed to grieve that.

Anger and sadness can follow each other in rapid succession. Once one is allowed expression, the other often follows. As long as our intention is to express our feelings to gain a greater connection with others and to support our spiritual evolution, expressing them provides us with insight and an opportunity to practice the art of communication courageously.

Working with Fear—Rick Quits Smoking

We commonly think of fear as a feeling. But fear is not a primary or pure feeling in the way that anger or sadness is. Most fear, in its essence, is a form of muddled thinking attempting to suppress primary feelings.

Rick, a thirty-five-year-old engineer, wanted to quit smoking. I was struck by his cool demeanor. Although he was asking my help with an intimate problem, his opening handshake seemed formal and stiff. He outlined his thoughts matter-of-factly. "I know intellectually that smoking makes no sense but I love the taste. I grew up with cigarettes and I like smoking—the sensation in my lungs, the way it feels, everything." Catching himself romanticizing about cigarettes, he smiled sheepishly. "It's going to be tough to quit. But I've got to. My kids are getting older and that stuff can kill you."

Rick tackled this problem in the same systematic manner that he approached other problems. He picked a day to quit, paid lip service to the emotional difficulty he might face, and then took a final inventory of the positive and negative effects of tobacco. One bright Saturday morning shortly after he started seeing me, he quit—cold turkey.

All went well for the first few hours. But as the day and night wore on, Rick started to experience strange and uncomfortable feelings. By Sunday morning, this intelligent, highly rational engineer was acting completely out of character. He planted himself in front of the television to watch old reruns on the kids' channel. He barked at his wife when she asked a simple question. Finally, he felt a violent wave of anger and hatred rise up within him and he went into his bedroom to thrash his pillow and grunt out his frustration. "What's happening to me?" he wondered. He thought he was losing his mind. He knew quitting would be difficult but he was unprepared for the magnitude of his distress.

When the anguish reached a zenith, he lunged for a cigarette. The relief was immediate.

In the face of Rick's terror, his rational mind gave in. When Rick plopped into his seat the following week, he looked defeated. "What's the matter with me? I should know better. Dammit, I watched my mother die from lung cancer." His eyes moistened when he mentioned his mother. "My closest uncle died from emphysema a few years later," he added, shaking his head. Some people just can't quit, I guess."

"That's not so," I said. "You *can* quit smoking. You just went about it too quickly and freaked yourself out. Quitting is more complex than just picking a day and stopping. You've got to face those deaths, and talk about it. Your unfinished business with them is preventing you from quitting smoking."

"You think so?" He seemed surprised by the connections I was making.

"Absolutely," I said.

In the next several weeks Rick talked about his mother. His memories of her and his childhood left him feeling very sad. Occasionally he felt angry at her for dying from a preventable disease and for other ways in which he felt neglected. The more he talked the more he had to say. Sharing his feelings was strange and new and, for Rick, was the "action" component of his growth process. Faith in his own emotional health deepened as he pieced his past together. Soon we were also able to integrate some practical steps to help him stop smoking. Each week he cut back a few more cigarettes until finally, when he was down to ten cigarettes a day, he quit successfully.

Rick told me he was too scared to quit. What he was afraid of wasn't the cigarettes, but the painful sensations in his body that were mysteriously linked to the death of his loved ones. Those unacknowledged emotional scars threw him. If we put his fear under a microscope, we see three components: first a stimulus, then a physical reaction to that stimulus, and finally the rational mind's response to that physical experience. The stimulus was the withdrawal of cigarettes. The bodily reaction was pain in his chest. The mind's response to that pain was resistance, confusion, and dread.

Gibran wrote that "pain is the breaking of the shell that encloses your understanding." Rick didn't know how to think about his pain and understand it. His lack of perspective left him assuming something was wrong with him. When I tried to warn him gently in the days before he quit that it might be harder than he thought, he would hear nothing of it. (I knew something was suspicious because if he really thought quitting smoking would be easy he wouldn't have hired me in the first place.) When the pain built up in his chest he didn't know how to coach himself gently and wisely through it. Instead he assumed something was terribly wrong. The pain of nicotine withdrawal combined with the latent feelings of deep sadness to knock Rick out. Sadness, like anger, has physical manifestations. Rick, not expecting such intensity, became confused.

If a dentist is drilling on my tooth and I'm expecting pain, it doesn't come as a shock or alarm. It's normal and I endure it. But if the pain seems to come from nowhere, it's scary as hell. The first time Rick tried to quit, he didn't understand that he was feeling more than a nicotine withdrawal. The next time he recognized that he was also dealing with emotional losses; so he was able to stop the spiral of fear erupting within him and use his insights to relax himself. Looking back, he saw that his fear was his resistance to painful physical sensations—not a pure feeling as anger and sadness are, but a set of thought/feeling interactions in which his thoughts tried to push away and resist physical and emotional pain.

Rick reached for his cigarettes when he thought he was going out of his mind. Cigarettes became a metaphor for "You're all right, calm down, have a smoke and you'll feel better." Had he substituted the words, "You're all right; sure there's a little extra tension in your chest and mouth; just feel it and relax, you don't want or need a cigarette," he would have made it through those first few days. Those words would have reduced the tension and pain in his body. But he wasn't yet able to redirect his negative thoughts. His mind was stuck on the channel broadcasting "I'll go nuts without a cigarette." If you believe you can't live without cigarettes, as Rick started to think in the few hours after he quit, you'll be in terrible shape when they're removed.

Before we can offer ourselves these soothing, positive directives, we need to first *slow down*. That buys us time to examine our thoughts. Just as many baseball pitchers go into the clubhouse between innings to watch their delivery in slow motion so they can pick up subtle problems in their form, we must pay careful attention for any tension-producing attitudes that may be deepening our dilemma.

We don't often recognize the build-up in tension while it's happening. Not until a headache or upset stomach strikes several hours later do we know we've been unwittingly cultivating damaging thoughts. Slowing down allows us to pick up the problem early.

Patience and clear thinking require enormous discipline. With them we can feel our feelings and choose our thoughts. But our instinctual reluctance to feel the awesome grief and horror that are part of life on this planet should never be underestimated. Fear abides until we can feel not just our own pain but the pain of others as well. The well appears infinite. Fear, the spiral of resisting our painful sensations or acting unwisely with them, exists on level after level. When we climb to the top of the stairs we can relish our accomplishment momentarily but lo, we are now at the bottom of the next level. There fear is waiting for us again, so that we can sort it out, make distinctions, and feel our experience—all the while allowing ourselves to grow and gain insight from our experiences.

My role as a therapist is to help clients stop thinking that their fears must dominate them. Sometimes it seems that I do nothing else but remind people, in a thousand different variations, of this great truth. (One reason I became a therapist is because you teach what you want to learn!)

Adele couldn't stop herself from fighting with her ex-husband even though it terrified their seven-year-old daughter. They fought each time they exchanged their child. "Something snaps in me, and I just can't stop myself," she lamented. "He knows how to get to me and I feel helpless."

"Helpless is a thought, not a feeling," I strongly responded. "You're not helpless even if you are afraid. Try saying 'I am helpless,' and then afterwards say, 'I am powerful.'" As she tried that little exercise, she quickly realized that one statement had power and a ring of authenticity to it while the other sounded like an excuse that kept her stuck.

I took that insight a step further during a group therapy session. Could she walk around the room and, one at a time, look directly into the eyes of each of the other eight group members and state clearly, "I am a powerful woman and I will not fight with my ex-husband in front of my child"?

At first she looked at me like I was insane for posing such a difficult challenge. "I can't do that, Mitch."

"You can. It would be embarrassing and risky. But it sure as heck would be supportive and make it more difficult to fight in front of your kid."

"That's true," she admitted.

"How important is it to you to stop that kind of fighting?"

She was cornered. Her choice was between her shame and embarrassment on the one hand, and her anger at herself for damaging her daughter on the other. To her credit, she saw it and popped out of her seat. She took her time and made contact with each group member to express her commitment clearly. Not surprisingly, in the next few months, she reported that she no longer fought with her ex in front of the child.

If we think of fear as real, it is real. It leads to war, senseless killing, horrific destruction. But if we cultivate the idea that fear is nothing more than a thought interacting with an emotion, then we can gain a perspective that helps us reduce the fear. This is the essence of what Franklin Roosevelt meant when he said, "The only thing we have to fear is fear itself."

If someone is sad, I let them be sad. I encourage the expression of their sadness, so they can taste it, feel their loss, and hopefully recognize gratefully that sadness is the flip side of love. That which yields us sorrow today was once the source of our joy. When sadness is expressed purely, it has beauty because it reflects love.

Likewise if someone is angry, I encourage them to explore that feeling. I explore with them how they can express it constructively. Maybe it's "Check your appointment book each morning." Or maybe "It's your turn to do the dishes." Anger and sadness, when experienced fully and appropriately expressed, provide us with insight, wisdom, and accomplishment.

When my son was riding his bike unsafely, I was able to turn what would have been destructive anger into a healing grief. This was in part because both those primary emotions were familiar to me. I was not afraid of either because, through the years, I have practiced expressing both appropriately. The discipline of separating our thoughts from our feelings, and then further dividing feelings into primary and secondary categories, is a process that blesses us with many insights and ample opportunities for courageous action.

Gaining insight by separating our thoughts and feelings is a starting point. But insight comes to us from many other places as well. The next chapter focuses on the insights and actions available to us when we consider the matter of our integrity.

2

The Risk of Honesty

L ISA had great sex during only one short period of her life. She was finishing her junior year at college when she met Curt, a handsome graduate student on a one-semester internship at her school. Their chemistry was magical. Sparks flew as this couple, who knew their time together would be brief, discovered the unbridled pleasures the body can yield.

The following year Lisa met her future husband Bob. Like Lisa and unlike Curt, Bob was responsible and earthy. She knew he'd be a reliable husband and solid father. Now (ten years later) she is married, sometimes even happily, and has two children, ages six and four. She still reflects nostalgically and furtively on that most delightful and amazing time with Curt.

Out of the blue Curt contacted her recently because he was again coming to town for a few days. Passion hung in the air during their phone conversation, reigniting a thousand sensual memories. Thoughts of that college romance flooded Lisa's mind, revitalizing her senses. Electricity was everywhere. Too often, life with Bob felt cheerless and uninteresting. Curt's offer felt like a spring breeze after a long winter.

Should she have an affair? The question pounded in her head. Would that be a dangerous mistake? Or would the greater mistake be to regret forever that she didn't seize the day? Wasn't she entitled to great sex at least one more time? While her body ached with longing her mind was flooded with confusion.

Although not each of us has a Curt popping out from nowhere to entice us with an opportunity that weakens the knees, Lisa's problem is hardly unique. We all encounter major and minor risks on a regular basis. The way we choose to respond to these risks is what shapes our lives. Living well means risking intelligently and creatively.

Lisa wants to squeeze every last drop of joy from her life. And it is well that she should. Living to the fullest is what we all want. When we don't we're left with a gnawing sense of guilt and remorse. Self-recriminations and excuses fill our heads when we squander opportunities. Deep down we sense that our own laziness, lack of courage, or lack of humility is what robs us of our joy. But, like Lisa, when we try to live to the fullest, we inevitably confront a myriad of risks.

How does Lisa decide? As her therapist how do I help her? As her friend or mother, what do you tell her? If she's you, how do you choose?

"How do you feel about lying to Bob?" I asked her.

"Terrible. He doesn't deserve that. He's not a bad man. You know he drives me a little nuts sometimes, but he's not the problem. For God's sake we've been married for so long, I'm hungry for something new and different. I don't want a divorce, just a little excitement."

"So what's the problem?" I asked.

"You know," she looked at me with exasperation.

"You don't want to think of yourself as a liar?"

She shot back. "I don't want to *be* a liar. I've never lied to Bob before."

"So tell him what you want. Maybe the two of you need a break from monogamy? Maybe he has an ex-lover just a phone call away? Maybe he's doing it on the side and lying to you."

"You don't know Bob," she said, shaking her head. "He's Mr. Clean. Tell him—right. He'd flip out. I know that. He'd divorce me."

"Well, you would at least get your excitement. It sounds like your life is boring. I don't think you just want great sex. I think the ordinariness of your life scares you. You're starting to get a glimpse into the future, and there's a dullness to it that is deeply disturbing."

Lisa was quiet for some time. While I stared out the window and listened to the birds chirp merrily, Lisa closed her soft hazel eyes and clasped her hands over her face. Tears slid beneath her hands and I gave her some tissues. Then, in a much softer voice, she said, "I'm having some kind of mid-life identity crisis, aren't I?"

"You are." The switch in her tone made me feel immediately warmer and more loving towards her. "Another way to say that is that you don't know what you believe in. You're questioning your values."

"Yes. I would have said that honesty and integrity are at the core of my life. I have always prided myself about that. I was raised that way and I chose Bob because of his integrity. Now I'm confused."

"First I want you to know that I think it's great that you're questioning your values. A lot of people accept what they were taught and don't find out for themselves what they really believe. That makes for a dull life because it's like we're living someone else's ideas of who we are. Questioning our values ultimately makes us think. Maybe honesty *isn't* the best policy. Maybe the truth *doesn't* set us free. Before we can adopt these values, we have to experiment with them."

"So what are you saying? That I should try lying to Bob to see whether I'm happier that way?"

"Just the opposite. Why not start by asking Bob to come here with you? Do some therapy together. Explore your feelings with him. Learn to expand your relationship so he gets to know the parts of you that you've been afraid to share. I think your relationship is boring because you aren't as honest with him as you need to be."

"That would be hard," Lisa said.

"It would take courage," I affirmed. "But remember, Lisa, something isn't working. The longer you wait, the harder it gets. Right now you haven't slept with Curt."

"Bob would be really hurt if he knew how I felt. Really hurt."

"Your love for each other would be tested. The value and importance of honesty in your lives would be tested. You will both emerge with more insight into who you each of you is and into what you believe."

Lisa brought Bob the next week. As I suspected, Lisa's attraction to Curt stemmed from the lack of intimacy and intensity in her marriage. The fireworks began when Lisa revealed some of her hidden longings. At first Bob was furious. Although this couple believed theoretically in honesty, through the years more and more had been held back. It took many months of active therapy before Lisa and Bob were able to share all their feelings openly. Towards the end of our work I asked Lisa if she still thought about Curt a lot.

"Only now and then. I know I did the right thing—my relationship with Bob is so much better that I'm glad the whole thing happened. It would be nice to turn back the clock sometimes, but that's not how life is. You were right, the truth does set us free. It hurts, but it works."

The Power of Honesty

In the introduction I mentioned the Zen master who said that enlightenment, or peace of mind, requires an acceptance of reality, exactly as it is, in each moment. We cannot accept something we are avoiding. Dedication to the truth is essential. Lying obscures our perception of reality; telling the truth reveals it. Alleviating suffering is impossible unless we're willing to look directly at our pain and open our heart to accept it.

The story is told that soon after the Buddha's enlightenment his extraordinary radiance left people dazzled.

"Are you a celestial being?" asked one.

"No," replied the Buddha.

"Are you some kind of wizard or magician?" asked another.

Again the Buddha replied, "No."

"Are you a man?" a third person asked.

"No."

"Then who are you?"

The Buddha replied, "I am awake."

Awake means absorbed, alive, attentive, rapt, diligent, alert. To be awake is to be present to life, to embrace its joy and sorrow, its pleasure and pain, with dignity and peace; to neither push away hardship nor crave pleasure; to accept reality, now and forever, eyes open, exactly as it is.

Dedication to the truth releases suffering, because the process of waking up is painful. If your arm falls asleep, it becomes numb, heavy, and useless. As blood rushes through it again, there's pain. When your soul falls asleep, the waking up process is infinitely harder. One way to wake up is to practice the risky discipline of honesty. We will never know if the truth will set us free unless we try it.

Our lies, deceptions, and attempts to escape from reality are part of our strategy to avoid feeling bad. Sometimes the truth hurts. But lying gets us stuck. In our efforts to avoid immediate pain, we twist or distort reality. By sidestepping that pain we create two problems where there was originally one. Lying makes us nervous that we're going to get caught, so we institute a covering-up process to maintain security. Complications invariably set in—just ask Richard Nixon. What exhaust is to an automobile, anxiety is to lying and covering up—a natural and inevitable consequence.

Shortly before Kathy and I were married, my explicit commitment to not hold back my feelings or thoughts was put to a test. It came in the form of another woman whom I found disturbingly appealing. "Oh no," I thought. "I don't want to feel this way now that Kathy and I are building a solid relationship.

I hated feeling intensely attracted to someone else. Of course, I also loved it. I was smitten and torn. Jenean emanated a glamorous sophistication that Kathy seemed to lack. Attempting to attract her, I flirted and showed off one evening. But why? I didn't even know. Afterwards I became angry with myself and confused.

When I saw Kathy the next day, I was at first cold and distant. She sensed that something was awry, but however she tried to draw it out of me I remained aloof. My dilemma intensified. I knew that telling Kathy about my feelings would precipitate a long and painful conversation. I also sensed that the feelings towards Jenean were fed by secrecy and that speaking about them would somehow weaken and diminish them.

My commitment to Kathy started feeling like a trap. I didn't want to tell her about how I felt, yet I wondered if I was blowing my feelings for Jenean way out of proportion—I hardly knew her! My mind was simply fantasizing out of control. My real life was bound to Kathy.

"If you have a problem," I tell my clients, "and you don't talk about it, you'll soon have two problems." It was no coincidence that the commitments Kathy and I had made explicitly stated no secrets. My desires were testing me. Finally I began talking. I lashed out, no longer trying to cover up my anger. "You don't meet all my needs," I blurted out. "Sometimes I wish that you were very different."

Kathy may not be the most glamorous woman in the world, but she knows how to communicate. She listened well, giving me space to voice my concerns and then asked that I do the same. Not surprisingly she had her own list of grievances. As it turned out, I didn't meet all her needs either.

A heated exchange followed that lasted several hours. Issues that had been glossed over in the preceding weeks surfaced. We trudged through everything. The conversation was scathingly honest and refreshingly charged. A lot of primary anger that had been withheld emerged. The process of communicating bonded us. We were both giving up a lot to be in a relationship. How could it be different? But neither of us thought we'd do better with anyone else. As our talk winded down, we renewed and reiterated our commitment.

The following week I ran into Jenean and, to my great pleasure, found that my attraction had mysteriously vanished. As we chatted, I saw only another person, not a potential lover to impress. My desire for her, I realized, had been nothing more than some unexpressed anger toward Kathy that I had been dishonest to myself about.

Romantic love is primarily built on illusion and fantasy —not on reality. No wonder so many marriages fail—we don't know who our partners are or what they need, and we're usually afraid to ask. In addition, we fail to explore the depth of our own needs. Honesty undercuts illusion and allows us to look at life as it is. This is why the discipline of telling the truth leads into freedom.

The Confusion of Honesty

The desire to be trustworthy is basic, embedded in our psyche. We desperately want others to trust us. Intuitively, we know trust and happiness go hand in hand. The quickest way to insult anyone is to call them a liar. The irony is that we lie to appear more trustworthy. When reality marches in, we get caught. "I always feel like scum," a client lamented, "when my wife discovers the truth and my lie is revealed. Even when she doesn't catch me, I keep looking over my shoulder."

Just as Lisa was pulled in two opposing directions, so are we all. Fear pulls us away from honesty. Integrity pulls us towards it.

I watched myself unwittingly contribute to the corruption of my seven-year-old son's integrity one day when I picked him up from day camp. Hilly's lower half was caked with mud as he walked barefooted, carrying his mud-drenched sneakers, toward the car. "We played in the puddles after the big thunderstorm,

Dad," he told me with a huge smile on his face as I glanced amused at his appearance.

"I see that," I said, placing his sneakers carefully on a mat in the trunk. On the way home we stopped at the supermarket to pick up a few items. "Come on in. It'll just be a few minutes."

"I can't, Dad. I don't want to put on those muddy sneakers."

"You can come," I said, matter-of-factly ignoring any reference to his bare feet.

"No, Dad," he explained. "You know that big sign on the entrance door."

He was referring to the picture of two bare feet with a red diagonal line through them. "Those are adult feet," I said only half-joking. "No one is going to bother you."

Hilly didn't buy it. He hadn't learned yet that rules are meant to be broken. He felt strongly about obeying the law.

I felt at least that strongly about leaving him unattended in the supermarket parking lot. I thought of my other options. I could go home and get him clean shoes. I could shop tonight and forgo the mushrooms and parmesan cheese for tonight's spaghetti. Or I could force my kid to put on those disgusting sneakers (he who loves mud so much, anyway). I ruled them all out.

Hilly and I tossed the dilemma back and forth, each of us rigidly sticking to our position. Finally I got adamant and said, "Listen, just don't stick your bare feet into the lettuce and no one is going to bother you. *Come on!*"

There comes a time when it's unwise to argue with someone three times your mass, so my son reluctantly entered the supermarket. I thought nothing more of the incident until I picked him up at the comic book section (where he hangs out while I shop). He had lowered his sweat pants a little around the waist until there was enough slack to completely cover up his bare feet.

It was then that I realized how much his integrity mattered. A strong enough will finds a way. "Contributing to the delinquency of a minor," I thought to myself, musing over my son's ingenuity. "This is how children learn that honesty isn't important. And I make a living reminding people how much dishonesty costs them."

This story makes two important points. First, children have a natural desire for integrity. In a child's innate desire for nurturing there is no duplicity, shame, or confusion. They hate it when their parents fight and they love fun. In short, children can be trusted to be real and to be true to themselves. As adults we can't say the same thing. No wonder we resist growing up. The journey into adulthood is a journey out of innocence and honesty.

The second point is that as adults we often undermine our children's integrity and unwittingly move them away from a value they will need to make their life work.

My mom insisted that I be honest, that is, as long as it suited her comfort.

"Mitch, pick up the phone please; but if it's Natalie, tell her I'm not home. I don't want to talk to her."

Then there were times she would tell me in all earnestness, "Do as I say, not as I do." The message was, "I can lie, but you can't." I remember one evening walking into the kitchen after she burned something. She told me it was my fault the food was ruined because I had aggravated her earlier. What's interesting is that I remember the incident. I've probably forgotten trillions of interactions that occurred forty years ago. This stands out because I must have been appalled by the extent of my mother's duplicity.

As a family therapist I see parents lie unabashedly to their children repeatedly and then wonder in exasperation why their kids are not more respectful. No wonder honesty is not an ingrained practice, it hasn't been role-modeled for us.

Our innocent childhood souls, having been bombarded with a host of conflicting messages, move into adulthood in a state of confusion. After being deluged by lies, many of which are sanctified not only by our parents but by our church or synagogue, we become as confused about our integrity as the adults who helped us get this way.

These conflicts are stored deep within the body waiting to surface when a similar issue or feeling surfaces and pushes the right button. When people abuse their bodies, either by overeating or through alcoholism or drug abuse, or allow others to take advantage of them, it is because they are out of touch with their integrity. We have lost our self, our way. Instead of hearing a healthy, guiding voice within, we tune in to our fears and falsehoods.

In the course of Lisa and Bob's therapy, Lisa remembered that her parents kept secrets from each other. When she was a teenager, her father sometimes confided in her to the exclusion of his wife. She enjoyed some aspects of her secretive relationship with her father—it brought her closer to her dad—but she was also troubled by it. Uncompromising honesty was not a value he role-modeled for her.

By the time we reach adulthood and attain a perspective from which we can look at our lives, we're already programmed to avoid different parts of reality. Regardless of how careful or loving a parent is, all children become infected—though obviously some have the pattern more deeply etched into their characters than others.

This confusion between honesty and dishonesty becomes a decisive factor in the way we live our lives. We can choose to be courageous and tell the truth, or we can hide behind a culture where dishonesty is often the norm. When Helen Keller spoke of life as a daring adventure, she wasn't thinking of Evil Knevil riding motorcycles over mountain gaps. She was referring to the courage it takes to live honestly and fully. When Lisa chose to bring Bob into therapy and reveal more of herself to him, she was raising the tightrope—putting more at stake in her life. The rationalization that originally prevented her from sharing with Bob was, "I don't want to hurt him." She realized, in the course of our conversation, that that was her way of avoiding reality.

Sidestepping the truth is more common than most of us care to admit. The next section alerts us to the extent of our duplicity.

Why and How We Lie

A young child wrote to God, "Instead of letting people die and having to make new ones, why don't you just keep the ones you got now?" Indeed. The concept of death is sufficiently forbidding that many of us live lives of bustle and babble to keep from thinking about it. Only when reality hits, when a loved one dies or is dying, are we forced for a moment to confront our impermanence. Reality, in all its unromantic matter-of-factness, is often unpalatable.

A friend told me a story of a woman who lost her teenaged son in a car accident. On one level the boy's mother knew her son was dead and would never return. Yet she made his bed fresh each morning and set a place for him at the dinner table every night. This went on for years. She refused to speak to anyone about him, preferring to live instead in isolation lest someone disturb her fantasy. Her denial prevented the penetration of any information that she wasn't ready to absorb. The pain was too much so she blocked it. An extreme case, yes, but beware. Some form of this woman's denial exists in all of us.

In our terror and bewilderment we look towards a simpler, easier, make-believe universe where people find love at first sight and live happily ever after. We don't want to be reminded of our finiteness, our mortality, our pettiness, our powerlessness. No wonder honesty is difficult. Being honest about our pain means feeling it. The mother who lost her teenaged son sought to blunt the absoluteness of death in hopes of avoiding the fierce pain she knew would explode within her the moment she accepted his passing. Accepting reality means accepting pain.

A year after a client was unceremoniously dumped by his girlfriend, he still refused to say good-bye. "That would mean giving up hope, and although intellectually I know it's over I just can't face the pain yet." So my client lived in a fantasy. When he finally accepted the end of the relationship, he had twice the pain because in addition to his girlfriend he had lost a year of his life in useless denial. Avoiding pain prolongs it. The inevitable cannot be stopped.

Children lie to avoid real or imagined punishment and ridicule. One woman whose relationship with her parents was troubled admitted, "I used to enjoy lying as a child. It felt great to pull something over those stuffy, stupid adults. One day I believed one of my lies. I forgot I was playing a game. When it hit later I got scared, terrified really. I didn't know who I was. If I could lie and believe it then nothing would ever be real, nothing was solid." This woman had stumbled upon a crucial fact of human personality: After hearing and telling enough lies, it becomes difficult to know what is true and what is not. After a while we no longer notice our deceptions. They become normal.

Just as the Eskimos have a few dozen words for snow, their specialty, we have many for lying. There are rationalizations, fibs, feints, little white lies, excuses, cover-ups, outright falsehoods, lies of omission, vagueness, and many more—including several varieties of grunting. The following conversation illustrates the art of obfuscation.

"Peter," I asked my eldest son several years ago as he sat watching television, "have you completed all your homework?"

Forty-five seconds later after I asked again he finally looked up and hesitantly replied, "I'm not sure."

"Not sure?"

"Not sure, Dad."

"What would it take for you to be sure?"

"Well my friend David was going to lend me a book and I don't think he's home now."

"So you're waiting for David to come home before you finish your homework?"

"Not exactly."

"What, is it a long story, Pete?"

"It actually is, Dad."

This conversation or a variation of it can go on and on. I would love it if my son said point blank, "No, Dad, I haven't finished my homework nor do I intend to finish it tonight. However, you needn't be concerned: I'm taking full responsibility for my actions and their consequences. Thanks for asking."

Had my then-fifteen-year-old son answered this way, I would have been shocked. Honesty in communication is rare.

When a friend of mine who runs a large business read this story about Peter, he sighed and said, "Nothing is more frustrating at work than listening to people make excuses. I just want my employees to take responsibility and respond honestly to my questions. For God's sake, why can't people be straight?"

How often do we lie? When I ask this question at workshops, most in the group exclaim that with the exception of the occasional white lie they are high-minded, honest citizens. But as I expand on the nature of lying, heads begin to shrug and sighs fill the room as almost everyone realizes the extent to which they practice duplicity. I wish I had a nickel for each excuse I hear in a day:

"It would only hurt my wife if I told her."

"You look really great in that polka dot hat."

"I went off my diet today because my car broke down."

"He wouldn't understand anyway, it's not worth disturbing the peace."

"I knew I said I'd come over but I got so busy, I just didn't have time."

"I'll do it tomorrow."

On and on it goes. We fudge it. We don't say what we mean. We beat around the bush both consciously and unconsciously. And not just about the little things. Often, too often, after a loved one dies, family members feel remorse because they hadn't been direct and said "I love you," —the ultimate in straight talk. But so it is. Only as we recognize this can we remedy it.

The Obstacle of Complexity

One reason it's hard to be honest is that life is complex. Much as we would like things to be black and white, they aren't. We have five senses feeding data to us. We have thoughts and feelings coming in a constantly changing pattern. We have confusion about our motives and our intention.

Frequently couples come angrily into my office and offer contradictory versions of the same event. After listening to thousands of conflicting stories I have come to realize that the truth is multi-faceted. More than one version of a story may be correct.

I make a crucial distinction between *a* truth and *the* truth. *The* truth implies something absolute, moral, and unequivocal. Speaking this way usually sounds preachy, stuffy, and arrogant. Instead I try to stick with singular truths—perceptions that have a ring of authenticity and that help us embrace a situation. When we discover various truths about ourselves we become more honest, authentic, and trustworthy.

When I think of why I became a psychotherapist, for example, I can offer several contradictory explanations, all of which are true. I can honestly say that I entered my profession because I love people and have a genuine desire to contribute to the reduction of suffering on this planet. Sharing with and enjoying people is something that comes naturally to me. But I can also say that I became a therapist because I wanted to know if everyone else was as crazy as me. The isolation of solitary insanity scared me. When I came to this realization, about five years into my practice, I was both embarrassed and relieved. Embarrassed because it wasn't quite what I had said when asked why I was seeking admission to graduate school; relieved because I could admit, at least to myself, that I was getting at least as much from therapy as I was giving.

So two different views or truths are applicable; they can even be complementary. Maybe I can never know why I became a therapist or had four children. Maybe it would be arrogant to say we know the truth about why we fell in love, or chose a certain career, or had various difficulties. What's important is to respectfully gather data about our lives with an open mind and heart.

By honoring the complexity of life we gain an appreciation instead of a dread of our dark side—what Carl Jung referred to as our "shadow." Our fear of this shadow often has us concocting myths and fantasies about life that have little to do with reality.

In my late adolescence, for example, I attended my first funeral. A relative had died. After listening to his eulogy, you would have thought he was the kindest, most generous and loving man who had ever walked the planet. It was laid on pretty thick. Several days after the funeral my dad was moping around the house and grieving. My mother let him have it. Her message went something like this: "He was a bastard. He screwed you out of money and no one liked him. Let's stop this false mourning." Yay, Mom. The truth in her words lifted everyone's spirits. When we hear *a* truth it leaves a powerful impression.

Although I know it's not in good taste to say nasty things about the dead, the extent of hyperbole in the funeral was what got to me. It emanated fantasy and denial. There are two sides to every coin. Even then something in me didn't like absolutes in this world of relativity.

Elisabeth Kubler-Ross said, "I'm not OK, you're not OK, but that's OK." The order is crucial. Peace or "OK-ness" is not reachable without first acknowledging our problems and travails. Just as an alcoholic must admit to drinking in order to mobilize internal healing forces, we must recognize the extent to which we shy away from the whole picture before we can accept ourselves peacefully.

Looking Good and Being Right

Cliff and Harriet were having another nasty fight in my office. She was tired of his volatility and anger. He thought she was selfish and didn't care about his deeper needs. I was getting bored and disgusted (some primary anger arising): We'd been over this one too many times. Instead of talking to each other, they talked to me as if I were a judge. I couldn't get them to stop interrupting each other, or to find any validity in what the other was saying. They interacted with a complete lack of respect.

Finally, rather than have them fill my ears, I decided to fill theirs.

"One Zen master," I began, "said you get married to practice dying. Since you'll one day have to give up everything—your family, your friends, the sunshine, your likes and even your dislikes—you might as well use your marriage to start practicing." I told Cliff he would have to give up the picture of a wife so tuned in to him that she could anticipate what he's feeling lousy about. His job was to accept Harriet as she is. He could make requests, but he needed to stop demanding that she be more caring and then using her inadequate response as an excuse for his belligerence. (Men get angry when I tell them that their marriage isn't going to work unless they give up their anger, or at least the bulk of it, which is mostly secondary false emotionality.)

Turning to Harriet, I said, "I understand that you can't stand his volatility. But if you slowed down and thought about some of what you do that he considers provocative, you'd see why he thinks you aren't caring enough. You need to wake up and recognize how you aggravate him."

Then I told them both, "As I listen to each of you, I understand why you're so frustrated with each other. I feel anger towards both of you because you'd rather be right and look good in front of me than recognize that fighting doesn't work. Neither of you is willing to give up your righteous position and listen even a little from the other person's point of view. You won't give the other person what you want to get—some kindness and respect."

This couple was more interested in arguing facts to prove a point than in honestly examining themselves to see if some common ground could be found. If either party had honestly talked about their loneliness or pain there might have been a breakthrough. What I realized from talking with them is that when it comes right down to it, we lie in our relationships for two reasons. We want to look good and we want to be right. We need to recognize this and cut it out. The choice is often between being right and being happy.

Being a marriage counselor is like trying to get the Israelis and the Arabs to trust each other and see that hatred doesn't work. After so many years of accumulated hurt, the cards seem stacked against us and we operate on habit rather than with clarity and respect. A Buddhist scripture states:

Hatred never ceases by hatred.
Only by love is hatred appeased.
This is an ancient and eternal and universal truth.

I can't think of anything better to remember as we struggle with others and ourselves in our attempts to be honest.

3

The Wisdom of Respect

To ACCEPT reality as it is, we must first respect it. Respect is the art of bringing loving and kind attention to whatever we are facing in life, and then behaving appropriately. Respect requires not only attention but also a willingness to listen to our intuition as it lets us know how to respond. When we are being disrespectful we bring out the worst in others because we are not seeing people for who they are. Conversely, when we interact respectfully we bring out the best from others and ourselves.

The process of respect begins in childhood. When children experience pain they want comfort, which may come from just a simple acknowledgment of their pain. I have watched in amazement as a simple kiss to a bruised knee immediately releases a child's anguish and sends the toddler merrily along. If I kiss or bring kindness to my own pain instead of cursing it, a similar freedom results, and the pain no longer binds me. The German psychologist Alice Miller calls this phenomenon "witnessing." When children do not have their pain witnessed, lasting scars are produced. Even great traumas can be healed if parents can lovingly and wisely witness their child's pain with great respect. Respect often translates to listening with kindness and acceptance.

People make a lot of noise when they are not being heard. "Sound and fury" Shakespeare called it. Much suffering, perhaps all suffering, stems from not being listened to, heard, and acknowledged—in short not being respected. Respect is to our spiritual bodies what food and air are to our physical bodies. It's the spiritual equivalent of money—something you can't get too much of because if you do, you can always feel good by giving it away.

When my third son, Jake, was three, Kathy and I were visiting with friends. Jake was upstairs with Rebecca, our friends' daughter. We were hanging out in their living room. At one point Jake came tearing down the stairs, crying almost hysterically. As Kathy stood up, Jake flew into her arms.

"What's wrong, honey?" she asked several times. Jake was too upset to respond. Undaunted, Kathy kept asking questions. "Did you hurt yourself?" Jake shook his head. At least now there was some response. "Did Rebecca hurt you?" Another head shake. "Did you get scared?" No response. "What scared you?" Still no response. "Did you think we had left?" Upon hearing the explanation that matched his experience, Jake immediately nodded his head, stopped crying as if on cue, jumped down from his mother's arms, and went back upstairs to play. Even before Kathy added that we would never leave without first talking to him, Jake was transformed into a happy camper.

He had been heard. His pain, which he couldn't articulate at three, had been labeled accurately and acknowledged. By matching the correct label to the experience, a process that required some trial and error, he no longer felt scared or isolated.

As Jake trotted off, the simplicity and profundity of the incident left me in awe. I had just watched in microcosm the heart of any respectful communication—one person taking the time to ask questions and listen fully until the other person felt heard. The interaction seemed natural. Of course a mother and young child would interact this way.

As we get older, it becomes harder to hear another's pain, harder to slow down and listen respectfully. This process doesn't apply just to young children. The most common complaint in marriage counseling is the isolation both parties feel from not being heard. We don't know how to label our pain accurately and then listen to it.

Carla was explaining to her angry husband, Simon, why she had had an affair. "I felt invisible. I didn't know if you saw me. I didn't know if anyone saw me, and the loneliness was so unbearable that I thought I was disappearing." Tears ran down her face as she looked fleetingly at her husband and then down at the couch. "I know it's not fair to ask you to understand this. I know you feel betrayed. I don't blame you. I would, too. But try to understand how terrified I was." I watched as she turned white with terror from talking about the experience. "When Gus [the man she had the affair with] started showing me some attention, I couldn't resist. I melted. I was drawn into it, my will left me." Carla broke into deep sobs.

This was not an excuse for her infidelity. She was talking about this affair years after the incident, because she had become strong enough to assume partial responsibility for her actions and because she had a genuine intention to revive her marriage. Her husband had previously been so angry and distrustful that he had never even asked the question she was now answering, "Why did you have the affair?" If he had been able to notice his wife's slow withdrawal years earlier, and to speak to her lovingly about how she was feeling, then she wouldn't have felt invisible in the first place. But this couple had no functional role models for relationships to show them what to ask each other.

Simon knew that Carla and he weren't getting along in the years before the affair, but he didn't know how to talk about it. He didn't ask: "Why are you growing distant from me?" "Are my actions pushing you away?" "Do you want to stay close to me?" Carla hadn't wanted to have an affair. In fact, she almost killed herself during it from the intense guilt, shame, and confusion. She had wanted to be heard. It took a year of therapy before this couple could start talking about how they felt about what happened years before.

Ask a hundred married couples if they think respect is a core value in a relationship, and they'll all say yes. Everyone wants to be respected, but most marriages are lacking in respect. Most of us pay lip service to respect, but when it comes down to it we don't know how to apply that value in our lives.

Respect requires that we allow others the freedom of choice. As obvious as this should be, it isn't. We are threatened by the actions and beliefs of others even if they have no impact on us. A father disowns his son because he is gay. A mother complains that her adult daughter's way of dressing is disturbing. A husband demands kindness from his wife instead of inviting it, and the wife lashes back by finding a different fault with him. The list of our disrespectful interactions could fill a public library.

Dialogue is an indicator that respect is present. When we communicate respectfully, we are more curious than self-righteous about why another is thinking or acting a certain way. When we're being respectful, we don't assume that we know what is in someone else's best interest. If we are sincere in our desire to be respected, we must practice respecting others. This chapter describes some of the communication tools that make this easier. Let's begin with a discussion about the art of asking questions.

The Socratic Method

Several thousand years ago, the Greek sage Socrates created a method of inquiry in which answers to life's dilemmas are attained through the asking of questions. The Socratic method of learning assumes that we possess an inner knowledge that can be accessed when specific questions are asked. All science takes place in this spirit of inquiry, this desire to know the truth. As questions lead to discovery, more provocative and subtle queries are generated, and the scientific process advances. The same process of questioning is also used in many spiritual and psychological disciplines. In Zen Buddhism, a student is given a *koan* or question upon which to meditate. The question doesn't necessarily have an answer; its purpose is to open up a process of internal discovery. In meditation, the student listens deeply to the inner self, the better to know how to resolve the *koan.*

Through the give and take of asking and answering questions we become more aware of our thoughts, feelings, values, and goals, as well as the steps we must take to accomplish these goals. Simply put, wisdom is a function of asking the right questions and listening well to the responses. A continuous feedback loop begins as each new answer reveals the next appropriate question.

A single question sets the context for all succeeding questions and responses that are at the heart of our psychological and spiritual growth. That question is: "What is genuinely in my long-range best interest and in the best interest of those around me?" If each of us kept this fundamental question ever present in our minds, we'd be a more loving and respectful culture. Sadly, we don't. We frequently engage without premeditation in actions that are detrimental or downright self-destructive, both to ourselves and to others. How many times have you heard yourself wonder with some disgust, "What was I thinking when I did that?"

Remembering to ask, "What is genuinely in my long-range best interest and in the best interest of those around me?" activates an awareness and caring that would otherwise be lost. It helps us have a better chance to listen respectfully to those deep needs within us that are often ignored, unheard, or unheeded.

Developing this art and skill of asking questions requires practice, but don't worry: Opportunities are virtually endless. After a friend had read a draft of this chapter she told me that the next evening her husband came home upset with one of his graduate students. She noticed herself start to go into a habitual communication mode of offering solutions to his problems.

Stopping herself, she decided to experiment with the Socratic method. She asked questions and listened. She let him figure out his own solutions. This took longer and required more soul searching on his part, but it was infinitely more satisfying and provided a better solution.

During a break from writing this chapter I walked into my dining room and found a small puddle of water on the table. I also discovered my seven-year-old son pouting in the corner, having just had a fight with his friend because his buddy threw a ball that hit him in the eye. I asked each whether they spilled water on the table. His friend answered no; Jake answered yes. Then I asked Jake if he would clean it. He did. Next I asked why he was upset. He told me that his friend wouldn't apologize. I asked his friend if he hurt Jake on purpose. His friend said no. So I asked if he'd apologize for hurting Jake accidentally. He told Jake he was sorry. Next I asked Jake whether he would accept the apology. He did and they were immediately lost again in play. I went back to writing and wondering whether we make life harder than we need to because we forget to ask questions.

Larry's story demonstrates the same principles with far greater consequences. A few questions can make the difference between harmony and despair.

In the course of his work with me, Larry revealed that he was having terrible fights with his father who lived with him. Fighting was especially fierce at meal times between Larry's kids, himself, and his dad. "Bring your dad in for a session," I said to Larry after listening to the issues. "I don't think he'll come," Larry replied.

"He'll come. Tell him you want to find out how to get along better."

The following week Larry showed up with Ralph, a big man in his late sixties with a pot belly and a weathered face. He shook my hand eagerly. He seemed flattered that his son wanted to talk to him. His soft blue eyes had a weariness that spoke of having seen too much suffering. When I asked the old man why he became so angry at dinner he paused for a long time, debating whether or not to tell his tale. What he said broke my heart and seemed unrelated, at first, to the fights.

"I was a prisoner at a Japanese POW camp during World War II," he began. "No one in the family really knows what happened to me there. I don't think anyone wants to know." Ralph paused. He needed some gentle prodding not only from me but also from his son. I asked Larry if he wanted his father to continue.

"Oh, yes." Larry said, his eyes glued on his dad. "Please continue." Larry knew that Ralph had been captured in the South Pacific, but no details were ever shared.

The old soldier continued. "We were put in a pen that wasn't fit for pigs. Slowly it became obvious that we were being starved. Until you live through it, you don't know what it means to be hungry. All I thought about was food. That was all anyone thought about. I hallucinated about food. Slowly I watched my buddies die, one after another. I don't know how I made it, but I did."

I could feel the silence in my body whenever Ralph paused. His story transported me to another world. Ralph went on for some time offering additional details of his captivity. His son looked on in awe through the eerie monologue.

At one moment, Larry blurted out, "So that's why you get so crazy when we eat!" Turning to me he said, "If any food is wasted or if it appears that any food might get wasted, Dad flips out. Now I understand it. I'm sorry, Dad, I'm really sorry."

Larry had often been furious that his father had insisted that he and his children finish each morsel of each meal. He felt like his father was being unreasonably controlling. Larry's eldest daughter couldn't wait to move out, and his son complained that he hated living with his grandfather.

After thanking Ralph for sharing his long-held secret, I said, "Now your story has been told. You may need to tell it again and again. But you also have to remind yourself that you're no longer in imminent jeopardy of death by starvation. So when food is wasted, you have to remember where you are and that what you want now is a better relationship with your son and grandchildren. It's not your job to worry about food anymore."

Ralph reinforced that idea. "I do want to get along with them. They're all I have now."

Larry moved his chair closer to his father, put his hand on his shoulder and said, "It's going to be better now, Pop."

Knowing how hard habits are to break, I added, "This will take practice and effort." I told Larry, "You have to help him and your kids put the past behind. Let your dad's stories be told. They are part of your heritage. As he is heard you'll all develop the kind of bond that makes fighting at dinner a thing of the past."

What troubles me the most here is that this old soldier could have easily died and never told his story. The way things were going, this son and grandchildren would have been glad to get rid of the cranky old man. Instead, they could now find a way to honor him. When there's a problem, people get angry instead of asking questions. Fairly simple questions brought the heart of the issue to light within a few minutes. If you watch good reporters and interviewers, you'll see the same phenomenon.

When I was a kid we played a game called "Twenty Questions." Someone would pick a person, place, or thing, and the others would guess what it was by using the art of deductive reasoning. With only a few questions, the most obscure topics were uncovered. Maybe all we need to do in life is play the same game. We could call it "Twenty Questions with Heart." Our curiosity is all we need to guide us.

Why don't we ask questions more often? Maybe we're lazy or impatient. It takes more work to ask questions. Maybe we're arrogant. We think we already know it all. Perhaps it's just habit. We're not trained to communicate this way. Perhaps we're just fearful of anything new. It takes courage to ask hard questions, wait and think about what you're hearing, and then ask follow-up questions.

Larry believed Ralph was a cranky SOB for so long that it melted his heart to realize that there was a reason behind his father's shenanigans at dinner. The risk of respect is that we will have to open our hearts and minds to a new level of compassion and a broader way of thinking.

Respectful Dialogue—The Story of Joyce

Joyce had been talking for about twenty-five minutes when I started getting sleepy. Usually I look forward to meeting new clients and offering them a taste of psychotherapy. I appreciate and respect the vulnerability that it takes to walk in cold and start talking about one's life to a total stranger. It's a privilege to play so intimate a role in people's lives, and that feeling is often heightened when I meet someone for the first time.

So I was surprised by my reaction to this heavy-set fifty-five-year-old woman who was laboriously describing her dysfunctional family. She wanted to tell me all the details of her sordid past—the drinking, the beatings, the angry children, the ignoring husband, the truly reckless behavior. I was beginning to understand how psychics and palm readers function—why they so often can sketch out a person's life and hardships after simply saying hello. Three minutes after Joyce came in, I felt like I knew her story. And now she was unfolding it, quite predictably, before me.

What isn't predictable, however, is how a person wakes up and transcends these patterns. This brings excitement and intrigue, mystery, and pleasure. But Joyce wasn't awake, nor did she appear to have much interest in awakening. She related to me flatly, without emotion, without eye contact, without *any* contact, as if she were speaking past me.

A friend had advised her strongly to come see me. Why was she here? What did she want from me? I asked. She ignored these questions, even after I repeated them several times. She was hell-bent on telling me a story that I sensed after twenty minutes wasn't going to help her grow.

She was taking charge of the hour, or should I say bulldozing her way through it, and I was fast becoming resentful. If I can't find something to like or respect about a client in the first hour, trouble looms ahead. I needed to take some drastic action. Trusting my instincts, and because I wanted to bond with this new client, I finally said. "Joyce, I want you to stop talking for a moment. I'm having trouble listening to you." Before I could t ake that pause and work it into a constructive communication, though, she was explaining how difficult it was for everyone to be with her. "Part of my pattern, dysfunctional family, you know . . ."

"Joyce. Wait! I want to talk, and I want you to wait until I'm done before you speak again. Can you agree to that?"

"Yes." Her momentum slowed down, at least temporarily.

"You're losing me and I don't want to get lost. Therapy is more than you speaking. It involves a sharing, a give and take, a relationship with each other." Since she had been speaking about how terrible her marriage was I asked, "If your husband were here and we asked him to list one aspect of your personality that most troubles him, what would he say?"

She cracked her first smile and sheepishly answered, "He would say I don't listen."

"Is it true?"

"Yes, that is true."

"Is that why you're here, to learn how to listen?"

"I guess so."

"I think so too, Joyce. Your life is important, and I want to get to know you. But you've been speaking at me, not to me.

"I assume that if I'm having trouble listening to you, you may not be hearing yourself, and no genuine dialogue is going on between us. Is it all right if I stop you whenever I don't feel connected to what you're saying?"

"I would like that," she said genuinely.

One of the reasons creating respect is difficult is that we play so many different roles in life. For me to be respectful of this client, I had to challenge her. Otherwise I wouldn't be doing my job and wouldn't earn her respect. We have to know what is expected of us in different situations.

To respect someone we must assume the best, not only of them but of ourselves. Because I genuinely wanted a connection, I was able to turn our conversation around by asking appropriate questions. The need for respect is universal. Everyone wants it. We bring out the best by asking questions—just keep playing twenty questions until the right question provides the opening you are looking for.

Respect and Bringing out Our Best

A lovely poster with a waterfall in the mountains reads "Today is the first day of the rest of your life." It's more than a great slogan or an over-used cliche, it's a truth. What I like most about it is that it respects the best part of our human nature— the part that knows we create our lives new each day. Tomorrow hasn't yet been lived and is an open book. There's an arrogance or disrespect in thinking that we know how we'll feel or what life will hold in the future. When I slow down, I can catch myself setting up problems or limitations that disrespect my nature as a creative, powerful being.

An attitude that predicts our future in ways we are generally unconscious about is a self-fulfilling prophecy. For example, I attended a seminar years ago in a distant city. Coming home late one evening I heard myself think, "Yuk, I'll be exhausted and useless tomorrow morning." Quickly I caught myself and asked, "How do I know that?" Was I programming a problem into my mind? I assumed the worst—that a few hours of sleep deprivation for one day would impair my functioning.

Determined to respect the energetic best part of myself, I used some affirmations to bias the mechanism of self-fulfilling prophecy in my favor. I repeated as I fell asleep: "When I arise I will feel awake and refreshed. Four hours of sleep," I assured myself, "is enough for tonight." I took a chance and respected my ability to adapt to a stressful situation. I set myself up for energy, not fatigue. The following day went well.

If it's hard to catch ourselves repeating subtle disrespectful patterns that affect only us, it's harder still to put this wisdom into effect in our relationships with others. That takes a willingness to listen respectfully and compassionately to someone else's anguish.

People in pain usually lash out randomly, and it's natural for others to feel personally attacked even if that was not the person's intention. This can trigger a spiral of animosity and disrespect. Assuming the worst is a deep-seated pattern. Children, for example, frequently blame themselves for a parent's turmoil, assuming falsely that they have caused a problem. "If I was a better kid," one child told me, "I don't think my parents would have split up." This fear-based, lifelong habit of always thinking the worst can dominate our personalities and have a terrible impact on the way we relate to others. If we can respect that good is latent in each of us, we set into motion the positive version of self-fulfilling prophecy.

When the Smith family trooped wearily into my office one cold winter afternoon, I could tell from the animosity oozing from each of them that my ability to be respectful was about to be severely tested. Mrs. Smith hadn't yet settled into her seat when she viciously lashed out at her thirteen-year-old daughter. The child made a face at her and hissed an ugly sound. Quite an introduction, I thought, "Only 59 3/4 minutes to go." Before that mess could be sorted, her husband erupted into warfare with their son, fifteen.

As the fighting intensified, I began feeling outnumbered by these four troubled beings, any one of whom would be a difficult client alone. I asked everyone to stop talking and to take turns answering the simple question, "Why are you here?" I listened for about ten minutes (it felt longer) as the different family members fought and interrupted each other, accusations flying.

It felt like spiritual war—their conflict against my commitment. I knew someone had to take charge. Interrupting their crossfire, I requested again that everyone stop talking.

"I'm confused," I admitted. "This isn't good. If I get confused, your time gets wasted. I'm sure you have better things to do than sit in a crowded office and throw accusations around."

My first task was to wrangle a personal promise from each of them not to interrupt me or each other. That took several   minutes to accomplish. Next I explained that they had come to therapy to learn how to communicate. (Here I was assuming the best. It was a courageous statement. Truly I saw no evidence yet to corroborate it.) The son immediately challenged me. Raising his hand and then shaking it like a young school child desperate for acknowledgment, he looked at me intensely.

I nodded in the boy's direction. "What?" I asked, knowing that real therapy was about to begin.

He was angry. "I didn't show up here to communicate. That's bullshit. I came because they threatened to ground me if I didn't come. I can't wait until I'm old enough to get the hell out of here and on my own. I'm not interested in communication. I want freedom." I moved my chair closer to Billy, the fifteen-year-old who posed this first challenge, and softly started asking questions. I was curious about his anger. He was hurt that there was so little warmth or good feeling in the family. He explained that he wanted to be out on his own because he had a life to live.

With the rest of the family sworn to silence, Billy and I conversed for about fifteen minutes about what he hated most in his world. As we talked, his suffering began to take a different form. Under his tough exterior lived a tender, gentle, young boy smarting with pain about the lack of warmth and good will in his life. I knew he needed to be heard before he could get in touch with any positive feelings.

Billy was enjoying the attention and respect our conversation offered him. His status as the uncommunicative bad guy was changing, which disturbed other family members who seemed to have a stake in maintaining the family's troubled status quo. Twice I had to silence his younger sister who wanted to tell her story. Billy, like everyone else in a family that doesn't communicate, had an enormous unfulfilled need to be understood.

Trouble came next when Billy started describing his relationship with his father. Mr. Smith could stand it no longer. He interrupted our conversation with a loud "Bullshit" (a word, I was beginning to realize, used frequently by members of this family).

Before Mr. Smith could unleash his objection, I reminded him firmly of his agreement to wait respectfully and not interrupt. Then I promised him he would get a chance to tell his story. "This therapy will work only if it works for everyone," I explained, "but that will take time. We can't untangle ten years of problems in sixty minutes. Trust me please and trust this process. This is Billy's version of reality. I understand that it isn't yours." I explained that if he could listen to Billy, he could at least find out how Billy's mind works and what Billy hears when people speak to him. "A healing for everyone can't occur," I said, "until each of you has a chance to share your pain and feel listened to. Please let me continue so we can find out what in particular is bothering each of you."

The father cooled off, allowing me to continue with Billy. The boy lived with two conflicting desires. He wanted to leave his family as quickly as possible and he wanted to stay and make it work.

I gave Billy's anger the benefit of the doubt. When he had said, "Bullshit," I heard OW! I assumed that his anger was a metaphor for his anguish. His facial expression and body posture revealed sadness and pain beneath his outward hostility. To stay connected to Billy and to bring out his latent commitment to cooperation, I kept a simultaneous "translation" running in my head, in which I changed his angry words at other family members into a description of his own pain.

Toward the end of our conversation I told him that I thought he would love to have a great family but had given up hope and developed a tough side to help him survive. "Before you give up," I asked him, "I would like you to try family therapy, not because you're forced to be here but because it may still be possible to learn how to get along with these people. I'm not sure yet what I have to offer you, but I would like you to stay so we can see whether some good changes can occur. You may even help soften up some of these other characters."

Billy agreed. His presence in therapy now became not only voluntary, but helpful: He now had a stake in making things work.

As each family member had a chance to speak (the introductions took two weeks), they united behind the single goal of better communication. Getting the four of them to agree on anything seemed like a miracle in itself. Positive movement was beginning and continued.

By holding the family to the value of respectful listening and by using the Socratic method to bring out the best in them, the power of respect took hold. Yes, it takes courage to assume the best and to maintain respectful guidelines. But as we train ourselves to listen and ask questions, we see that practicing what we preach is not so difficult and brings results that often go beyond our wildest imaginings.

Respecting Grief

Respect is difficult because it involves listening, and sometimes we don't want to accept what we're hearing—it's too painful.

As I lay down next to Hilly to say good-night once when he was twelve, he began to cry. "What's wrong?" I asked my normally good-natured boy as I wrapped my arms around him. His crying increased, but he said nothing.

"Talk to me, please, Hilly. I want to know what's going on."

"We don't spend enough time together, Dad," he finally blurted through his tears. "I feel like I never see you." I couldn't tell whether he was angry or sad, but as he repeated a variation on this theme I started feeling defensive and annoyed. He sounded angry, and I felt accused. We had just spent a week together on a family skiing vacation.

"Will anything satisfy this kid?" I wondered. I stayed silent and let him cry.

I suspected that the big fight we had only yesterday precipitated this problem. It was a fight that Hilly uncustomarily lost. Our disagreements usually end in peaceful reconciliation. Almost always we create compromises or reach a satisfying understanding. But last night's dispute ended in an ultimatum. Hilly was not living up to his agreements about the care of his dog, who pooped on the carpet while his master sat absorbed in the television. I had been furious. "Your agreement was to walk the dog regularly when you're home. Keep this up and the dog goes." He had known I was serious.

Hilly's body was still wrapped in mine as I waited silently. When the crying subsided, I asked him to tell me more. His desire to spend more time with me sounded strange. I didn't trust it. "When you say you want to spend more time with me, what do you mean, Hilly? Something else is upsetting you and I want to know what it is." I waited a little longer, sensing more was on its way. Another wave of tears heaved forth.

"I can't take it anymore," he blurted out. "I have so much to do, so much pressure. Everyone bosses me around. I wish I could be five years old again, when everything was easy. No school, no chores, just play. You and mommy weren't divorced. Life was so much easier. Now it's so hard, so hard." My son was lost in grief, his chest heaving in agony, his words barely audible through the sobbing. Over and over he repeated, "I wish I was younger, I wish I was younger." This was no manipulative temper tantrum put on for my benefit. Hilly wasn't angry with me; he was upset with life. Between the recent increase in his school work-load and the realization that his irresponsibility could cost him his dog, his emotions had completely overwhelmed him. His pain touched me, melting my anger, erasing my defensiveness. The harsh taskmaster within me, the voice of anger that might have said, "Stop shirking your responsibility, your problems aren't worse than anyone else's," gratefully was silent.

Hilly was in the midst of an identity crisis. I recognized the symptoms because I see them at work each day. Even though he was only twelve his experience was every bit as valid and as painful as any adult's. People enter therapy to redefine themselves, to clarify their expectations, and to set new goals. The process involves grief. Finding out who we *are* and what we *want* means giving up who we *were* and what we *had*. Hilly was adjusting to his new age and role, as well as to an enlarged share of responsibilities. He never had been twelve before and that scared him. I remembered similar feelings during my adolescence, when the world seemed large, cruel, and unbearably lonely. The worst part was feeling like I had no one to confide in, no friend or adult who understood.

As my son cried, I hugged him tighter. I was relieved to hear him express his pain, glad that he could share it. I knew the healing value that comes from full self-expression. Tears of empathy as well as acknowledgment began flowing down my own face. We stayed in each other's arms until he was cried out.

"I love you, Daddy," he said as I shared a few words to let him know how much I appreciated the courage it took for him to speak about his painful feelings so openly: "Life is hard sometimes. Very hard. But at least we love each other and we can share." Soon he was asleep.

Watching Hilly in the next few days, it was obvious that a weight had been lifted from his heart. He went about life with more than his usual zest and pep. He was a pleasure to be around.

Our communication that evening worked. It brought us closer and renewed his energy for the tasks of the day. Yet what had I done? I hadn't removed his pain or shielded him from the tough realities he faced. He still had to walk the dog, complete his homework, do his chores. What had orchestrated such a loving exchange?

The key to this success can be found in the listening. When Hilly told me that he wanted to spend "more time" with me, I translated his request to mean that he wanted "intimate time." Had I taken him literally, I might have planned a future outing. That wouldn't have satisfied him or released his pain. His words had fooled me at first. I had felt tense and uneasy. It took discipline to keep my mouth shut until I understood his true intention. By assuming the best, being patient, and asking questions, I was able to get to the heart of the matter. His words said one thing while his heart said another. Fortunately I had kept quiet long enough to listen to his heart.

Growing up isn't easy. Children get scared when they see what's happening to their bodies. Adolescents often do whatever they can to slow down the transition into adulthood. Instead of being aware of this grief and respecting it, they tend to be blind or impatient and assume some sinister plot. Pain is an immediate indicator that respect may be missing.

To respect something is to acknowledge its nature, to accept its reality. One respects a hurricane or lightning storm by behaving with prudence. Respect for fire means knowing its power. Respect in relationships means knowing that each person's true desire is for connection, for happiness, for relief from suffering. The power of respect brings out the best in ourselves and each other.

What we must respect, ultimately, is our fears. We hate being so afraid of life just as we hate other people for their weakness. But we are the way we are. Fear is built into the system. Disrespecting it makes it worse, not better.

This next story describes another typical day of parenthood. Sitting in a corner of our kitchen, I watched Hilly, who was about six at the time, reach into a pretzel bag and inadvertently drop one on the floor. Seeing the fallen pretzel as an opportunity to practice one of his latest passions, soccer, he kicked it around and finally guided it toward the goal, which in this case was the space underneath the refrigerator. With a last successful shot, he scored. The pretzel disappeared under five hundred pounds of metal and food.

"What are you doing?" I asked in amazement.

Looking at me with total innocence, he sought clarification. "What was I doing when?"

"With the pretzel. Why did you kick it under the refrigerator?"

"It fell on the floor, Dad, so I didn't want to eat it. You told me to throw away food that falls on the floor." Although I was taken slightly aback by his naivete and apparent innocence, my anger resurfaced. His action had triggered a negative attitude that sometimes takes hold of me: I begin to think that my children are part of a massive plot designed to make my life harder. I soon found myself acting out a role that I fully detest—that of policeman. "What is it with you?" I self-righteously shouted. "Since when do pretzels belong under the refrigerator?" My words and tone were in effect saying, "Why are you so bad? Why!"

As I looked at my son and saw his own fear and bewilderment, I realized that I was falling into the same trap that I exhort my clients to avoid. I had interpreted a situation with the least empowering assumption and was communicating disrespectfully. A wave of sadness passed through me, and I softened considerably. "I'm sorry, Hilly. I didn't mean to yell at you. The pretzel will rot underneath the fridge. Bugs will find it and eat it. It might stink. We don't want ants and other little creatures roaming around our kitchen looking for extra food." Ah, these points he understood. I realized that to a six-year-old oblivious to ants and odors, the space underneath the refrigerator seemed as likely a depository for a dirty pretzel as a garbage pail. After all, do you look regularly under your refrigerator?

My son was not trying to make my life harder. He was not being stupid, evil, or spiteful. He was using the six-year-old common sense available to him at the time to help him solve a problem. How easily I could have belittled or scared him—creating a downward spiral of guilt and resentment. At worst he was being lazy (a sin well known to his father). At best, he was being creative. It was up to me to interpret the pretzel either as a symbol of my child's playfulness or as an assault on the house's cleanliness.

Respect operates on numerous levels, but its power is to take our ordinary interactions and impart a mindful or sacred quality to them. What we are ultimately respecting in ourselves is the spark, the essence of divinity that lives inside us. By living with respect, we strengthen our intention to honor that which is sacred in each of us.

4

The Mystery of Responsibility

Responsibility through Vision

One day a man walking along a path fell suddenly and unexpectedly into a treacherous pit. Livid and disoriented, he flailed out of control around the pit's murky bottom. "Who did this to me?" he screamed. His fury prevented him from noticing any escape routes. Only after his yelling subsided did he calm down and search for a way out. With great difficulty, he found one.

The next day, the man was walking the same path. This time he caught a fleeting glimpse of the pit as he approached it. But it came too late, and he fell again. Yesterday's flailing and cursing were repeated. Again his vile temper and rising fury made it harder for him to escape. He was a master at making a bad situation worse. Finally he remembered the path and climbed out.

On the third day, this fellow again walked the same path. This time he saw the pit clearly and shouted a warning: "Watch out for that blasted hole." But curiosity overwhelmed him. He felt intrigued and fascinated, repulsed and disgusted, but finally compelled to explore the pit's outer edges. As he bent closer to look, he fell in again. By now he was getting better at climbing out. He spent less energy blaming the universe for his fate and more on climbing. He emerged from this third descent with a shake of his head and even a wisp of humor at his own stupidity.

He realized then that even on the first day he had noticed the pit before he fell in, although it hadn't registered consciously.

The fourth day, walking along the same path, the man slowed down noticeably as he neared the pit. The mysterious feeling of being drawn uncontrollably towards the hole struck again, but this time he was able to stop and just feel it. An acute sense of helplessness passed through him, but he kept a respectful distance. He managed, albeit with great difficulty, to walk around the pit.

The next day the man took a different path.

To one degree or another, we're all like this guy. We don't see problems before they arise, and when they hit we waste precious time blaming others and complaining to the wind. We don't take full responsibility for our experiences.

This story had a happy ending. The man learned from his mistakes and changed his stupid ways in five progressive steps. It should be that easy for the rest of us. It isn't. Most of us are stuck like the man on the second or third day, struggling blindly to extricate ourselves from something we inadvertently keep stumbling into. With slight variations many of us have the same problems now that we've had all our lives. They keep repeating because we don't see to the heart of our problems. If you pull a weed without removing its roots, it returns.

At the heart of our problems lies a failure to assume responsibility—first, for our lives in general and second, and more specifically, for how we think about different situations. We create attitudes by the way we think, and attitudes determine everything. They determine how we assess our feelings.

I may be standing in the front a room, for example, about to give the most important talk of my life. My heart is pounding. My attitude can be, "How awful, I'm sure I'll screw this up and make a fool of myself." Or it can be, "What an exciting opportunity! I'll make the best of this." Although I have no immediate control over how rapidly my heart is beating, the attitude I choose to adopt might well affect whether the pounding of my heart increases or diminishes.

Our choice of attitudes determines whether we see life in terms of opportunities and possibilities or in terms of what can go wrong. Control over our attitudes gives us power. In many situations, the particular perspective we embrace determines the quality of our life. At every moment and in every circumstance, we have the ability to rise above life's catastrophes and shine.

There's an old expression: When life hands you lemons, make lemonade. Sure, some of us are born richer, more beautiful, or more talented than others. Yet each human being has to face the primary challenge of death, and each of us has to face the almost unbearable sorrow of loneliness. Life often feels like it's too much, that we can't get beyond our circumstances. But anything is possible when we are willing to train ourselves systematically to think differently.

The one constant in life is our own presence. Nothing has ever gone or ever will go terribly wrong or right in life without our steady presence. When we look back—either from our present vantage point or from our death bed—we're left with intuitive knowledge that this is/was our life, and we alone are responsible for what we created.

Assuming full responsibility for our lives doesn't exclude the presence of a higher power. Appealing or praying for mercy, compassion, strength, or inspiration may indeed help us contact those qualities; but it's up to us to make the appeal. God helps those who help themselves. Jesus said, "Seek and ye shall find, knock and the door will be open." Our willingness to take responsibility for our seeking and knocking is at the heart of the matter.

I mentioned that one Zen master described enlightenment as accepting reality exactly as it is in each moment. By thinking critically, we can cultivate and deepen an attitude that makes acceptance possible. Accepting something doesn't preclude a commitment to also making changes. In fact, we make changes effectively only after accepting the presence of problems. To give up alcohol I must first accept the presence of a problem. Then I can mobilize my energy to successfully change that problem. Before tackling life's external circumstances we must first recognize that our attitudes or thoughts of acceptance are at the crux of our well-being. The Dalai Lama said it this way:

> *The purpose of life is to be happy. As a Buddhist I have found that one's own mental attitude is the most influential factor in working toward that goal. In order to change conditions outside ourselves, whether they concern the environment or relations with others, we must first change within ourselves. Inner peace is the key. In that state of mind you can face difficulties with calm and reason, while keeping your inner happiness.*

To live happily, to live constructively with risk, to create a world from our own imagining, we must take full responsibility. This self-evident truth is the cornerstone of all that follows.

Rising above our circumstances and turning lemons into lemonade sounds great; but you may be wondering, "Does this guy live in the same world I do?" How does a concentration camp victim rise above circumstances? How does a ghetto dweller or an innocent child who has suffered horrible abuse face the steep challenges of life? Certain obstacles seem impossible to overcome. Am I offering too simplistic a solution?

The suffering in the world is immense: Not for a moment are these words about taking responsibility meant to further victimize or blame those unable to free themselves. For many, this concept is scary or incomprehensible. Others may find it inaccurate because it seems to negate the role that luck—good or bad—plays in life. Are we not entitled to be victims if we're unlucky and lose a limb, or a child, or have a terrible disease?

It's understandable that people adopt such attitudes. But just because life is tough and arbitrary, that doesn't mean we should give up control over our destiny. Many strong feelings and thoughts about our suffering may be based in illusion. Self-deception is part of the human condition, and we often need reality checks to make certain we're seeing life clearly. For thousands of years the world was considered flat; it does look that way. Even if an entire nation believes a lie, the lie doesn't become true.

If we jail a thousand people unfairly, ninety-nine percent will complain and curse their fate. Ninety-nine percent will say they are victims of circumstances, bad luck, or persecution. Understandable, yes. But what about the one percent who don't think that way? What about the one percent for whom unfair hardships don't represent a time for complaint? What about Mahatma Gandhi, Martin Luther King, or Nelson Mandela, who never let their incarceration foster lasting bitterness? What about Helen Keller, who despite being deprived of her senses, was able to live a rich and fulfilling life? These human anomalies are worthy of study. From them we can learn the value that comes from not succumbing to a victim-mentality that believes we're not responsible for the dignity and quality of our life.

This is why the Dalai Lama stated that before we can change circumstances outside ourselves we must first focus within. An example of recognizing that the power for transformation lies within comes from Mohandas Gandhi who once stated that he had three enemies—the British empire, the Indian people, and himself. Of the three, he considered only himself as a formidable opponent. Only he stood in the way of achieving his goals. He knew that he alone was responsible for life. And I bet he experienced more peace and freedom in jail than most of us experience roaming the world. His life and the lives of others who overcame their circumstances shine a path to all of us who get stuck in life's arduous circumstances.

Theoretically, we are responsible for our lives. Gibran takes the theory to the extreme when he writes: "The murdered is not unaccountable for his own murder / And the robbed is not blameless in being robbed."

Responsibility is an ideal, and as an ideal it can become a discipline. As a discipline it can bring meaning and structure to our lives. Over time, through self-discipline, we can face our struggles with greater equanimity. With discipline we can view our pain from a different perspective. Instead of thinking of it as an enemy or obstacle to our happiness, we could embrace Gibran's view of pain:

> *It is the bitter potion by which the physician within you heals your sick self.*
>
> *Therefore trust the physician, and drink his remedy in silence and tranquility:*
>
> *For his hand, though heavy and hard, is guided by the tender hand of the Unseen,*
>
> *And the cup he brings, though it burn your lips, has been fashioned of the clay which the Potter has moistened with his own sacred tears.*

A clear definition of responsibility is difficult to make. Sometimes we define things in terms of what they are not. The truth cannot always be spoken. Rather than to abstractly define what responsibility is, the rest of this chapter describes what it isn't. Approaching it this way, we can alert ourselves to the core value that may be unspeakable or indescribable but which we can recognize when we see it.

An example of getting to the core by stripping away the nonessential can be seen in the realm of art. As Michaelangelo stared at a slab of marble, he saw David. His job was to remove the parts of the marble that were not David. Slowly, as the nonessential was removed, David revealed himself. Michaelangelo knew intuitively when to stop chipping. As we discipline ourselves to not engage in activities that are irresponsible, our responsible self emerges.

Responsibility Doesn't Complain

Complaining is never responsible. It is incompatible with critical thinking. It is a waste of time, but one we invariably indulge in. It is so deeply ingrained in our personalities that it is almost impossible to fully eradicate and difficult sometimes to even identify.

The childhood version of complaining is whining. Whining seems to be a natural tendency that takes vigilant parenting to slowly eradicate. I can't stand it when my kids complain, so to make my life easier (and ultimately theirs) I make life uncomfortable for them when they do it: just another service provided by their dad. The adult version of whining is complaining; just as no one enjoys a whining kid, complaining adults are tough to be around.

Complaining alerts us, like a flashing light on a car's dashboard, that a problem needs immediate attention. Sometimes we need others to help us see that warning and then heed it. Shortly after Kathy and I were married, for example, I complained on two successive days about some minor medical ailment. She asked me to either do something about it or stop talking about it. Her message couldn't have been clearer. Although startled at first by her directness, I took it as a wake-up call. Idle negative chatter isn't welcome in our home.

Another time Kathy was going off to buy a small piece of furniture. She invited me to come but I don't like shopping, so I declined.

"If you don't want to come, does that mean you trust me to pick this cabinet out?"

"That's fine," I said, "You can do it."

"But this also means that if you don't like it after I schlep it home, you don't get to complain about any aspect of it—not its color, its price, or its workmanship. You've lost your vote."

Suddenly I had a desire to go, which alerted me to how much complaining plays a part in life.

As a therapist, I am often called upon both to alert my clients to their unconscious complaining and to train them to take responsibility for their speech. Here's part of a dialogue with a clinically depressed young man who complained incessantly about the intrinsic horrors of the world.

I would invariably ask him, "How's it going?" at the beginning of a session. Phil usually answered with a grunt, "Life sucks."

After getting nowhere for several weeks, I reframed my approach. "Does life suck," I asked him, "or does *your* life suck?"

"Life sucks! This world has nothing good in it."

"My life doesn't suck. I'm pretty content. Life is rich and interesting. Isn't it more honest to say *your* life sucks?" Phil looked confused and maybe curious. Sensing I was on the right track, I went into a little speech. Slowly, emphatically, passionately, I said, "Look outside, do the trees suck? No, the trees are just trees. Does the sky suck? No, the sky is just sky; it doesn't suck or not suck. Even nasty people are just nasty people. They don't suck, they're just nasty. Because many people have been nasty to you doesn't mean life sucks. It means you don't have the tools to deal with nasty people and difficult situations. Life doesn't suck. What sucks is your lack of tools to deal with tough situations. If you want to get out of your depression, you'll have to force yourself to stop complaining about your fate."

Like many of us, Phil hid behind existential ideas that allowed him to escape personal responsibility. Much easier to pontificate about the ills of the world than to fight one's personal depression by changing dysfunctional ways of thinking!

Our complaining is so much a part of our background noise that we need help to recognize it. At group therapy, a man who had been a member for two years was bemoaning his tough life.

John was lonely, yet he made no attempts to meet women. He worked too hard but wouldn't say no to his boss. Several folks challenged him to take positive steps. One even offered to introduce him to some of her single friends. Each request was fielded with a ready excuse. When the group become frustrated by his evasiveness, I stepped in and said, "It seems like you're so used to carrying this burden of loneliness that you no longer want to put it down. Your identity has merged into that of a complainer; you're not seeing yourself in perspective."

I asked John to try an experiment. Instead of sitting with the group, how about if he spent some time walking back and forth behind everyone carrying a wooden chair? The chair would symbolize the burdens and complaints that he accepted as his daily lot in life.

He could have refused or sat down at any time. Instead, he paced back and forth for more than ninety minutes until the group ended. At first the other members were disturbed by his awkward removal from the circle and his pacing. But within minutes everyone became accustomed to it and we carried on normally. Now and then we checked in with him. Sometimes he felt angry, other times bored or lonely. But John kept carrying his burden as he watched the group silently from beyond the circle. His behavior that night in group paralleled his life: the lonely outsider complaining to himself that life doesn't work.

Over the next few months, a major shift became noticeable. Gone were his complaints and traces of sarcasm. Life began going much better. Mr. Negativity acknowledged that thinking of himself as a complainer had provided a rude awakening. "I didn't realize what I sounded like. I found out that after you stop complaining outwardly you start feeling better all around."

Sometimes it takes a physical symbol to alert us to our complaints.

Ironically, what we complain about is the reality that we *are* responsible for our life. Although none of us wants to become a slave, it's far easier to think of ourselves as innocent victims or powerless peons. Then if life goes poorly it's not our fault.

Responsibility is practically a dirty word in our culture. My thesaurus lists only the following synonyms for it: blame, burden, culpability, defect, fault, guilt, misdeed, misdoing, and onus—not a single positive connotation. With a cultural heritage like this working against us, no wonder we're struggling!

The extent to which responsibility has become synonymous with burden is revealed by an exercise I sometimes conduct at workshops. I ask the group, "If you won the lottery, would you continue working the same job? Do you *get* to work or do you *got* to work?" If you are in the great majority who would quit their work, then you know an undercurrent of complaining and dissatisfaction must be present. I once went to a lecture by Elisabeth Kubler-Ross, who started her talk to close to a thousand people by asking, "Who doesn't like their job?" More than half the audience raised their hands. "Quit it," she challenged them. "Don't spend your precious life doing something you don't want to." A milder way to say that is, "Use your complaining to recognize that you have a problem, and then start training yourself to make a change."

Try this experiment: Ask a few people you know if they want more responsibility in their lives. Eyes will roll. Most people already feel their plate's too full. Ask the same people if they want more opportunities to make their lives richer, more satisfying, more joyous. Everyone wants that. But we don't realize that we can't create better lives without taking on more responsibility. I'm not talking about more burdens or things to do, I'm talking about a deep-seated willingness to look our complaints, petty ailments, and minor grievances in the face and realize that they all trace back to choices *we* made; choices that no one forced upon us.

When my first son was born twenty-three years ago, my dad asked me if I felt an enormous sense of responsibility. My life as a parent was just beginning, and I lightly answered "No." I was clueless about what lay in store.

Three and a half years later, when my second son arrived, I was overwhelmed by a sense of opportunity and responsibility. I remember walking out into the woods less than an hour after Hilly was born, plopping down beside a tree and feeling wave after wave of emotion. I was crying in prayer that I would be worthy of what was being presented. I was keenly aware of the link between responsibility and opportunity.

Ultimately what we take responsibility for is the choices we make along our path. Life brings hundreds of choices, big and small, each day. Taken together our choices comprise the essence of our life. Choice is sacred. Upon its altar millions of lives have been sacrificed. We have fought wars whenever we believed that our democratic freedoms to pursue our happiness were endangered. To think of responsibility as a burden or hardship is to demean the sacrifice of those who have fought to protect our freedoms.

Ventilation vs. Complaining

A client once asked: "You listen to people all day long. How do you tell the difference between a genuine sharing from the heart and useless psycho-babble?" The question involves a basic distinction between complaining and ventilating. Complaining is pollution, an unnecessary dumping of toxicity into the atmosphere that takes the form of denying responsibility for the quality of life. Ventilation, on the other hand, is an intimate sharing that connects us to others and validates our pain. At its best, ventilation becomes witnessing. If a holocaust survivor is sharing his or her anguish, you as the listener are bearing witness, and the interaction between the two of you is sacred. During traumatic events, those who survive often bolster their will to live by thinking of sharing and becoming a witness for the event.

The difference between ventilating and complaining is

sometimes subtle and subjective. Listening to a client share a story, I often feel deeply moved. The communication allows the client to re-experience and heal wounds from the past. I feel privileged to share someone's vulnerability and am moved by the risks he or she is taking. Such conversations are invigorating. At other times, however, while hearing a story I become impatient, bored, or disconnected. Stop this useless complaining, I think. My compassion isn't awakened. The client's words sound shallow, unrelated to their gut-level experience of the incident. Yet if I were to write down the moving words uttered by one client or the annoying sentences uttered by another, I'm not certain there would be much difference. The content of the sharing—the description of the past incident—may be nearly identical.

At the beginning of a new group series, for example, a woman shared a painful, moving story. Her vulnerability was obvious and other group members bonded with her easily. However, in the following weeks she repeated the story again and again. The vitality and vulnerability were lost. What once was a beautiful sharing came to sound more and more like complaining.

All of us possess an invisible bullshit meter that intuitively alerts us to inauthentic communication. Developing the bullshit meter's accuracy takes discipline and practice. The bullshit meter scans for qualities of authentic sharing—respect, clarity of intention, honesty. When I'm not sure if someone is dumping, or if I'm complaining to myself, I start asking questions about the purpose in speaking.

Sheila was describing in a couple's session how her husband Bob often throws mini-tantrums when he can't find things. "Little things set him off. He stormed around the house the other day looking for his keys. He does that all the time and I feel kind of sorry for him—he lives in turmoil."

"You felt sorry? Are you sure that's what you were feeling?

Why should you feel sorry for his irresponsibility? Sounds to me like Bob wasn't ventilating his frustration at the loss of his keys; he was complaining and throwing a tantrum so you'd feel bad for him and he could avoid taking responsibility for his lack of mindfulness."

Lots of us make noise to create a distraction after we screw up. But noise makes no difference. Heading for a confessional after we've sinned often comes not from a genuine desire to change destructive patterns but from a desire to get permission to sin again.

Sheila looked dazed by my response. "I do hate that he acts like a spoiled little kid so much of the time. He's always losing some essential piece of his life and carrying on. He's not a peaceful person to live with."

"Does that leave you feeling more sexually attracted to him or less?" I asked, throwing in a twist. (I knew this couple was experiencing sexual difficulties because their attraction had faded.) At this moment Bob, who had been sitting passively through the discussion, perked up.

"I guess I've been programmed to feel sorry for him. But it's not what I'm really feeling. I'm kind of disgusted. You mean it's okay to ask him to stop complaining?"

"Is it okay for your kid to throw garbage out the window when you're driving down the highway?" I inquired. "It's all right to ask Bob to internalize his complaints unless speaking them out loud has a clear and positive purpose."

If I'm not sure if something is a ventilation or a complaint, I ask, "Are you telling me this to share, to feel intimacy, and because you want to get this off your chest so we can be closer?" If there's some positive intention and some sense of risk and vulnerability, then it's ventilation. If I need help, I ask for clarification. If this sounds a little laborious or artificial, it can be. But it beats being confused and resentful, which is how Sheila felt around Bob much of the time.

"Bob," Sheila finally concluded. "It's true. Your complaining is a big turn-off. I want you to stop."

Bob was angry at first. "I'm not the only one complaining. You do it, too. What's good for the goose has to be good for the gander."

I chimed in. "If you guys can call each other on your complaining with respect and caring, then not only will you both be better off, your kid will also be the winner. Kids hate listening to their parents complain.

We leak energy when we complain. With some self-discipline, the same sloppiness that keeps Bob misplacing his keys could be changed into becoming better organized.

Responsibility Doesn't Blame

As we take more responsibility for our lives, something curious happens: Not only do our own lives transform, the lives of those close to us are also touched. If there's hope for our inhumanity to each other on this fragile planet, I believe it rests in the gradual spreading of personal responsibility to encompass larger and larger circles. "Do not doubt the power of a few conscious individuals to change the whole world," stated Margaret Mead. "Indeed, it is the only thing that ever has."

When personal responsibility expands into including others, we have social responsibility. This concept is far more complex than personal responsibility because there are so many extra variables. Hard as it is to figure out my own needs, it's vastly more complex to assess my responsibility to my family, my community, and my planet. Paradox and confusion abound in the realm of social responsibility because we can never assume responsibility for another—that would violate the sanctity of free will. But we can make a difference. We can create an environment that makes it easier for others to bloom, just as fertile soil produces greater crop yields.

Complaining prevents us from taking personal responsibility

for ourselves; blaming impedes us from being socially responsible. Blaming others is never inspiring. It is never helpful. When Jesus was asked whether a criminal should be stoned to death, he replied, "Let he who is without sin cast the first stone." On another occasion he said, "Take the log out of your eye before you take the mote out of your brother's."

This story about a recently married couple demonstrates some of the complexities and possibilities that emerge when we expand beyond the realm of individual responsibility. Steve and Bea brought one child each to their newly constituted family. Steve's daughter, ten-year-old Sandra, was having problems. She blamed her new stepmother, whom she disdained, for the dissolution of her parents' marriage. She also disliked her older stepsister, Beth, who in her eyes was a carbon copy of her mother, Bea.

Living with each of her biological parents only half the time was oppressive for Sandra. She longed to roll back the clock to a simpler time of mommy and daddy under the same roof. After some time Sandra's powerlessness erupted into covert violence. She began to destroy some of her stepsister's best clothing. She cut an arm from Beth's favorite sweater. She slashed her most expensive blouse. A gash destroyed Beth's favorite jeans.

Beth was horrified when she discovered her mangled clothing. She showed it to her stepfather and mother, who were outraged. When confronted, Sandra defiantly let them know that she had indeed slashed the garments. She remained cold, detached, and unrepentant.

When I met Sandra at a family session, she initially could not explain her destructive behavior. But when she realized that in the safety of my office her dad would listen to her and that no repercussions would follow her revelations, she began talking about her fear of his anger. She cried as she described her dad's temper tantrums. Steve knew his relationship with his daughter was tempestuous, but he was oblivious of the extent to which his daughter feared him. Over a period of several weeks, we negotiated an agreement that called for him to stop screaming at her and for her to stop destroying property. She also agreed to pay for some of the damaged clothing.

At first, Steve was irritated because I seemed to be letting his daughter off the hook while putting him on it. Instead of exacting restitution from his daughter, I asked him to take responsibility for how his own behavior was contributing to Sandra's distress in a way that wouldn't be clear until it stopped. Children sometimes have to act out in bold, destructive ways to get attention. Sandra felt blamed and afraid during her father's outbursts, which only made things worse.

In the next two weeks Sandra's previously open hostility to everyone in the family subsided. Several times she saw her father struggle to keep his part of the bargain. It moved her. "Daddy really tried hard to control himself this week," she beamed. "He didn't blast me once." And she had tested him, too. By taking responsibility for his share of Sandra's distress, Steve made it easier for his daughter to feel heard and loved. Her destructive actions covered up an enormous grief she felt about the loss of her family. Some of that grief could now be addressed.

Few things in life are more satisfying than being able to contribute to another's well-being. Sandra was visibly moved when her father psychologically stretched himself to control his temper. If he could change, she knew she could also. It turned out that she stopped her destructive behavior as soon as he stopped his. Contributing to others' well-being begins as we take care of our own personal business.

Steve was not responsible for his daughter's change in behavior, but his contribution made the difference. When he stopped being so angry at her he made it easier for her to take responsibility. Sandra was inspired to change, but it was she who ultimately made the choice. In other situations I've seen kids with pretty good parents not stop destructive patterns.

As a therapist, my job is to create a safe, healing environment in which clients can grow more easily. Just as some salespeople far outsell others, some therapists are more successful at helping clients. The line of reasoning in this chapter holds me responsible for my client's growth. And in a general sense I am. But thinking this way can also lead to a terrible trap where responsibilities become burdens and I can be manipulated by clients. It would be foolish for me, for example, to let a client who is having a hard time ruin my day. I can take responsibility for being inspiring or creating an environment which optimizes growth, but ultimately responsibility for others has a limitation. Hard as I may strive at being a successful professional, I must always remember that ultimate responsibility stops with each individual.

Blaming others doesn't work. When Hilly was ten, he lost a new jacket. When I heard about it I started yelling at him. "Dad," he said, "I already feel awful about it. I don't understand why you're yelling at me. It's not going to bring the jacket back." I shut up immediately, ashamed at myself. The incident remains etched in my mind. Blaming doesn't work.

Guilt Is Not Responsibility

Where guilt is, responsibility is not. Guilt masks true feelings. Steve felt guilty that his divorce had put Sandra under so much distress. But instead of taking responsibility for that pain and being there for her to grieve, his guilt led him to avoid acknowledging her needs. Long before his daughter took scissors to any garments, there were problems Steve was ignoring. Often when Sandra was difficult, Steve felt guilty. Her pain reminded him of the failure he felt from the dissolution of his marriage. He knew he had let his child down. Not surprisingly, it was hard for him to find balance in his discipline. Sometimes he was far too lenient—shying away from confrontation. Other times he was too harsh.

Like complaining and blaming, guilt is a clear sign that we

are misunderstanding responsibility. Guilt is not a feeling. Stop yourself each time you "feel" guilty and ask yourself if you're thinking about responsibility in a mistaken manner. In Steve's case, his "guilt" masked a tremendous well of unacknowledged and unexpressed grief stemming from the divorce.

If I "feel" guilty for spending so much time away from my family while I'm writing this book, it's because I haven't clarified my priorities or made clear agreements with my wife. It would be a misnomer to say I "feel" guilty—really I would be "thinking" myself to be guilty. Our guilt serves as a warning light alerting us that we're not communicating precisely. All of this is easier said than done, because sometimes excruciating feelings block our critical thinking.

The way we play out the dance of guilt and responsibility is at the core of how we think about ourselves. The stakes are so high that it's easy to not think clearly.

When Norma accidentally ran over her beloved dog, she felt unable to forgive herself until she was first punished. "How much punishment," I asked her, "do you need before you can make peace with yourself?"

"But I *am* guilty," she replied.

"I don't know if you're guilty. I do know that your dog ran under your car and was killed and that your guilt won't bring him back."

"But if I don't suffer for this, how do I know I won't stay sloppy and make another horrible mistake like this again? Do I need to run over my other dog before I learn my lesson?"

What could I say? We do indeed have painful lessons to learn. And sometimes pain is needed to wake us up. I could only implore Norma to be kind to herself as she experienced her pain so that her lessons would be learned as quickly, as efficiently, and as compassionately as possible. It wasn't really guilt she was experiencing, but agony and grief that life is sometimes so cruel. When going through personal torment, blaming ourselves doesn't help; but we do need to learn our lessons. Guilt prolongs suffering. Since we have to suffer, let's get it over as quickly as possible.

The line between guilt and responsibility is tough to draw. A painful personal experience once helped me intuitively understand their relationship. When I was twenty-two my mother took her own life. During my childhood she had had periodic bouts of severe depression. Perhaps because she no longer had children dependent upon her she gave in more readily to the suicidal impulses that accompany severe depression. The experience changed my life. Although quite close to my mother, I was so engaged in starting my own adult life that I spent very little time with her during her final depression.

Twenty years after her death, I attended a nine-day intensive silent meditation retreat. The retreat provided solitude and safety to explore the recesses of my own pain. Towards the end of the retreat, during one meditation, I had a direct experience of empathy that connected me to the horror I'm sure my mother felt immediately preceding her death.

I knew at that moment that had I been a more loving and available son I could have prevented her suicide. I wasn't blaming myself or feeling any guilt whatsoever, although it may sound that way. I simply "knew" that people kill themselves because they feel unbearable loneliness and despair and that if I had been more present, and knew what I knew now, I could have prevented her death.

The experience was accompanied by an intense emotional release, but it was not debilitating. In fact, since that experience ten years ago I have been more at peace with my mother's death. It was the absence of guilt that allowed me to penetrate beyond the thought or concept of blame so that I could take full responsibility for the extent of my grief at my mother's passing. I believe the experience has also helped me to be a more compassionate and skilled therapist when I work with suicidal clients.

Burden Is Not Responsibility

Responsibility is not a burden but an opportunity. A fateful example of this comes from the world of politics. When I was an adolescent, Lyndon Johnson became president following Kennedy's assassination. I remember listening to Johnson speak movingly of the great burden of responsibility he felt as president. The theme recurred in all his addresses. When he looked the camera in the eye and told the nation he felt burdened, he wasn't acting.

In retrospect, it's easy to see that his confusion between burden and responsibility hampered his clarity about Vietnam and many of his other duties. During that era, Johnson had trouble sleeping at night. It was common for him to wander into the War Room in the White House basement and start micro-managing affairs at 4:00 in the morning. He became obsessed with small details. My hunch is that the overwhelming burden he felt prevented him from finding the best perspective to conduct foreign policy responsibly. The confusion between burden and responsibility can throw us off balance, causing our actions to be harmful.

I was sitting with a couple who had been married for twenty-five years. They had raised two children and at last had achieved financial stability. They had suffered together, laughed and loved together. Now it was their turn to enjoy the easy life they so richly deserved. But they were torn apart by petty bickering.

I listened as each recited their grievances, each convinced that the other was somehow responsible for their pain. I was struck by how unwilling each was to recognize that their own pain related to how they communicated.

"Don't you want your lives to be lighter and easier?" I finally asked them with a mixture of curiosity and deep sadness. "Blaming doesn't work. You guys need to lighten up."

Lightness became the theme of the session. Repeatedly I asked them to phrase their questions with more good will and kindness. During the hour, their blame-reflex softened. It reminded me of a couple who, after eighteen months of therapy, summarized the therapy with this simple remark in our concluding session: "When it comes down to it, you have reminded us to be kinder to each other. That's why our marriage is working so well now."

Life is hard enough. My practice is to face difficulties consciously but to also seek out the easiest path. My children will attest to my vigilance in that regard. When Jake was six, he got really annoyed with me one day for encouraging him to make his life easier. "Dad, what is it with you?" he said in exasperation. "You're always telling me to do things the easy way. What's so good about easy anyway?"

"Hmph," I said. "Maybe you have a point. Why make life easier? The next time you want a glass of water, instead of just hopping up to the sink, fetching a glass, filling it with water and drinking it, why don't you first take the glass and bang it on your head, then throw it down and break it, then sweep it up, and then go get a different glass and fill it with water? Why make life easier? Do it the hard way!"

Jake started laughing as I went through this ludicrous scenario. He got my point. But it's an easy one to forget. Easier is better as long as we're not avoiding anything. Taking responsibility is easier!

Another story. As I reread this chapter I noticed that the words "take responsibility" are continually repeated. I'm obviously attempting to hypnotize you, to plant those words into your subconscious so that they magically appear whenever you get stuck. I do in fact practice this as a technique with my clients and kids.

When Hilly was fifteen, Jake was only three. At dinner time Hilly would sometimes allow his little brother to get on his nerves. He hated the way Jake fussed about food. His parents, he thought, were not being sufficiently parental. Hilly sat next to me and each time Jake annoyed him I placed my hand gently on his leg and stroked it softly, slowly repeating, "Relax, Hill, you'll live longer that way." At first he resisted my bizarre response. In time it amused him.

Several months later while Jake was having a mild fit at the dinner table, Hilly sat oblivious to the fracas. As he ate his dinner, he looked up suddenly. He remembered midway through Jake's whining that it was these kind of incidents that used to bother him. He volunteered, "You're right, Dad. It's not my problem. I might as well relax. Thanks for all those reminders." With that he went back peacefully to his food.

Common Boundary

A final paradox about responsibility takes us to the common boundary between psychology and spirituality. Although I don't make a hard distinction between psychological and spiritual growth, the two do have different aspects that can be confusing.

The discipline of psychology focuses on building a person's confidence and sense of worthiness. This is accomplished as we take responsibility both for the circumstances of our lives and for our reactions to them. A self-actualized person, the epitome of psychological health, is completely responsible.

The purpose of spiritual practice can be defined in opposite terms. Instead of strengthening the individual's sense of self, it is designed to enable the individual to dissolve the feeling of separateness into the larger spiritual body of God.

Before we can dissolve our tightly-held sense of ourselves, we have to possess something worthy to release. My eighty-three-year-old father inadvertently offered a great example of this dynamic when he mused recently about the unimportance of money. After speaking in a manner previously uncharacteristic for him, he added, "I guess you first have to have money before you can realize its insignificance."

Similarly, before you can give yourself up to God you have

to build your ego strength so that you have something worthy to offer. Another way to say this is that we can't give something up until we first have it. Similarly, in order to face death graciously, I suspect we have to live fully.

I've noticed a mysterious energy as I approach deeper levels of personal responsibility. Instead of reinforcing my own individual sense of self, my personal will feels like it merges with a larger force of will, commonly called God's will. Another paradox: Attuning ourselves to God's will becomes gradually available as we assume more personal responsibility. As we get stronger, it allows us to disappear into something larger. Thus the link between psychological and spiritual growth.

5

The Power of Commitment

SPIRITUAL and psychological growth comes about when our insights combine with appropriate actions. The power and depth of our insights relate directly to the amount of courage, honesty, respect, and responsibility we bring to our lives. The force that empowers these virtues and that brings value to life is commitment. Everything we cherish—our family, friends, work, and interests—is important because of our commitment to it. Take away this profound human ability to make commitments and life loses meaning—it becomes shallow and empty. Without commitment, love loses its power, depth, and soul, and our communication falters.

Breaking a commitment is like stabbing ourselves. With each self-inflicted wound a piece of our integrity and self-confidence withers. When we dishonor our word, we no longer know who we are or where we stand. As we stop believing in ourselves, others stop trusting us and a downward spiral of personal doubt and confusion gathers momentum. The only way to halt and reverse the fall is to re-establish our integrity by demonstrating an ability to make and honor our commitments.

Thoreau once said that for every thousand people hacking at the branches of evil, only one chops at the root. If there are 999 fools for every wise person, that's because we let our confusion and fear about commitment stop us from getting what we want. Chopping at the roots of evil is a difficult and rigorous practice for which we have been poorly trained.

There's nothing sexy, glamorous, or enticing about making and keeping commitments. It's something adults do. Children can be trained to clean their rooms, do their homework, and be at least outwardly respectful. But they are not yet capable of creating commitments.

Commitment builds the bridge that allows our visions to manifest as reality. Like bridges of concrete and steel, its foundations penetrate deep into the earth. This chapter sheds light on the subject of commitment and offers some valuable tools that can help you create powerful commitments in your life.

Ultimately our commitment must be to life itself. Sally, twenty-eight, had been in intensive therapy for more than eighteen months when she called late one Friday evening. "Why should I go on?" she stammered. "All I can see ahead is pain." As a child, she had been raped and assaulted by her brother and abandoned by her parents. Now she and her ex-husband fought constantly. Precious few positive memories were stored in her heart.

Still, Sally was a survivor. She had extricated herself from the abysmal environment of her childhood, found a good job, and made some friends. She started therapy to get help with fears that sometimes overcame her and prevented her from sleeping well. As she explored the past, she saw that her childhood insecurities were haunting her. The more she remembered, the more shocked she became by the extent of her trauma. She was stuck between the proverbial rock and hard place. "I know if I don't face my past and grieve my losses I'll never get through my fears. But the more I remember them, the more it hurts." And she was tired of hurting.

"I want to kill myself, Mitch," she told me that Friday evening. "I don't believe I can ever live a happy life. I'll never be able to trust a man, and life will be mostly pain. I've never felt this bad."

"It sounds like two things are bothering you," I softly

responded. "First, you're remembering past trauma and talking about it stirs up the old feelings. You pretended for the last ten years that the past didn't really affect you. But it does."

"It really does get to me. I see why I put it out of my mind, and sometimes I wish I could go back to my old unconscious self."

"You weren't so happy then either, Sally. That's why you started therapy."

"It's true. But I feel hopeless, Mitch."

"But in addition to the trauma, Sally, there's a bigger problem. You have no container to hold that pain, no context that makes sense. So with every new revelation, you get confused about whether it's worth it. Most of the time while we're working, you're wondering in the back of your mind if you should go on. The suicide option is always open and it tugs on you. To survive your childhood you needed an escape plan. You kept a back door open. But now that open door lets in a dangerous draft that's makes it impossible for you to think straight. More than being scared and feeling hopeless, you mostly sound confused."

At this point Sally got angry at me. "I am confused. Why shouldn't I keep suicide as an option? You'd do the same if you had to go through what I have to face."

I ignored her anger. "I want you to commit yourself to six more months of therapy without any consideration of suicide. To work through this pain, you can't keep thinking that maybe you can escape it."

"Six months! No way. I'm not making new commitments. You want too much from me," Sally shouted, getting still angrier. She had never let herself become this emotional with me before.

"Six months. You can close the suicide option for six months. I know you can. I'll be here for you, you can trust me. Your pain isn't the real problem. Your lack of commitment to yourself is what's missing. That's your real pain, and it's making you scared and confused."

"Too much," she said stubbornly.

A long silence ensued on the telephone. I knew that Sally was also testing my commitment to her. I lay down on my bed and let the phone rest near my ear. No one had ever been there for her, and I prepared to wait it out.

"Why are you being like this?" she asked me.

"I don't want you to die. I want you to live. I believe in you. I believe you can work through your grief and live a good life."

"You're just saying this because you get paid to do this."

I laughed. "Quite a job, huh?"

"Do you really care about me?" Sally asked. She was risking more vulnerability than ever before.

"Yes," I said genuinely.

After a long time, she said, "I still don't want to give you that commitment."

"You're not giving it to me, you're giving it to yourself."

"I can't."

"You can."

There was another long pause, maybe two minutes of silence. Talking to a suicidal person requires a lot of patience and faith. Finally Sally sighed, "Okay, you win. I won't kill myself in the next six months."

Sally was angry with me after that call. She felt like I had been mean to her. She said nasty things about me to her friends. But she kept her commitment and continued her hard work. Her life became more painful but less confusing. In the months that followed, she let herself experience the primary emotions of anger and sadness that had been so much a part of her childhood. Her fears and confusion diminished. A year later she looked back upon that decision as a turning point. She never noticed when the six-month period was up, because by then her commitment had grown. As hard as life sometimes was, she never again doubted her core commitment to herself.

For Sally the issue was one of life and death. She had to give up her option to die, an option many of us hold on to secretly.

Everyone struggles with commitment, but usually the battles are more subtle and less defined. When I made the issue so distinctly black and white, it was easier for her to see her choices.

Commitment affects the daily activities of our life in a thousand different ways that we seldom notice. Without commitment, there would be no will to exercise, eat well, or say 'No' appropriately. We'd be afraid to have emotionally honest, respectful, and responsible interactions. We'd shy away from risk and conflict because engaging in them would no longer be safe. Couples would not be able to face their issues without fearing that their problems would destroy the relationship. Without commitment, we would have no capacity to create a spiritual life. Commitment is so essential to our lives that we sometimes lose perspective about it and forget that at the heart of every commitment lies a choice.

Choice

Commitment represents the end of a childish notion of freedom—that's its price. The moment a client accepts an 11 A.M. appointment, all other possibilities of how I can spend that time are gone. Since I can't be in two different places at once, with commitment comes a loss of options. The deeper the commitment, the greater the sacrifice; and the greater the sacrifice, the more intense the resistance and fear. Personal courage is needed to meet the demands that commitment brings.

A commitment to marriage, for example, means saying goodbye to sexual experiences with other partners. A commitment to children implies years of profound daily sacrifice. Commitment can sound like the end of fun. Look at some of the synonyms for commitment in the thesaurus: burden, debit, dues, duty, confinement, obligation, liability. No wonder commitment seems so formidable and forbidding: We think of it as the end of freedom.

Thinking this way is understandable but only half the story.

And the less important half at that. Commitment breathes love and joy into life. A relationship without commitment lacks intimacy and lasting pleasure. Withdraw commitment from your family, friends, or job and the value of these treasures vanishes instantly. Making a commitment kills only one element of freedom—the chance to do something different with our time. But freedom isn't just keeping physical options open. It involves a way of thinking and acting that maximizes the choices we exercise over all the elements of our life.

Commitment opens the door to true freedom. Commitment always involves choice. To create a commitment presupposes that we have the freedom to not make the commitment. Commitments are never automatic. They are mindful decisions that take root only after different options are considered.

A colleague who smoked incessantly once defended his habit by proudly stating that he chose to smoke. What baloney! "You can only choose to smoke," I reminded him, "if quitting is a viable alternative. Could you just as easily not smoke tomorrow as smoke?" He grimaced and walked away. Giving up his habit was only a theoretical option for this man deeply addicted to nicotine. He didn't choose to smoke; he smoked because he was stuck, because his habit was bigger than him, because he was unwilling to tap into the energy of commitment and exercise his true power of choice.

My colleague's dilemma was made worse by his unwillingness to be honest about his addiction. Instead he rationalized, falsely labeling his cigarette habit a choice. He wasn't willing to confront the *lack* of freedom his fear-driven habits and addictions caused. Experiencing our freedom requires confronting fear and facing pain. New choices appear only if we allow ourselves to think freely and openly even as we consider difficult or excruciating options.

As fear is rolled back, more choices become available. Acting in our long-range best interest becomes easier and more natural. If my colleague broke through his addiction and realized not smoking was as viable an option as smoking, he would choose to quit because in the long run quitting makes more sense—even if he enjoyed tobacco as thoroughly as he insisted. Although fear always plays a part in life, it doesn't have to run counter to our common sense.

The commitment-making process leads us to think of freedom in terms of ideas and attitudes, not simply in terms of physical attainments and possessions such as the right to smoke. No wonder commitment helps our lives to work: It pushes us beyond the material world and leads us to the spiritual life, where the non-tangible forces of love and spirit are paramount. Commitment is seen as a burden and obligation only when we focus upon what has to be given up on the material level, instead of appreciating the love that can be gained. By focusing on the beneficial elements of commitment, we tap into a power within ourselves to evoke joy and fulfillment. Focusing on the loss of physical freedom commitment brings produces the opposite effect—it reinforces our identity as materialistic beings afraid our wealth or comfort will slip away.

Most of us were not trained by our parents in the art of creating and keeping powerful and appropriate commitments. Even if we had been, the process would still be difficult. The remainder of this chapter explores the components of the commitment-making process. We look first at desires and the importance of knowing what you want. Next we take a look at the three steps that turn desires into commitments. Finally, we look at what can be done to break through any remaining confusion.

Knowing What You Want

Commitments start out as desires. This is a problem because desires often conflict and run us ragged.

I want to be nice. I want to be tough. I want to be loved. I want to be left alone. I want more money. I want more time. I want more sex. I want, I want, I want . . .

The Rolling Stones reminded us of what we've always known: "You can't always get what you want." But we don't believe it—in fact we resist it. Instead of wisely prioritizing our goals and weeding out clearly unattainable or counter-productive desires, we indulge in unrealistic hopes and fantasies until they've locked us into a classical no-win confrontation. The bottom line is that we can't have it all if two of the things we want directly oppose each other. Our unwillingness to let go graciously of some of our desires has turned this would-be happy song into a dirge.

We don't get what we want because we don't *know* what we want. We haven't been trained to listen respectfully to our *needs*. So we have trouble separating the gold from the mud. We accept confusion as a fact of life. The creative skill of prioritizing has been all but abandoned in our lust for a quick fix or easy life. Knowing which desires to chuck and which to elevate to com-mitments becomes an important key to happiness.

Patty, thirty-five, is a single mother whose boyfriend drives her crazy.

"He wants too much from me. If I let him, he'd take over my life."

"So what do you do when he gets too pushy?"

"I act like a cold bitch. That keeps him away for a while."

"Great. Is there a more respectful way you could communi-cate your needs?"

Patty and Sam had been breaking up and getting back together for eighteen months. Each separation lasted two to three weeks, then one or the other would get lonely and rekin-dle the fire. On again, off again.

"You need to decide if you want to be in this relationship. Each time you withdraw he gets needier and the cycle repeats."

"I know I do that, but I'm not sure he's the right guy for me. You know how different we are."

"What do you *want*, Patty?" My question couldn't have been more direct.

"I want an easier relationship."

I looked up to the ceiling, and began talking to God. "One easy relationship, please. Patty doesn't want to work too hard in this one." She laughed, and I added, "That really is the problem. You want it easy, but relationships are hard. Before getting out, why not work hard for a while? Then, if it doesn't work, you can at least know that you did the best you could."

We can't make commitments until we see the outline of our struggle clearly. In the mad swirl of desires, it's often hard to think straight enough to reduce our problems to the desires that are in conflict with each other. The first task is always to gain clarity about what we want. Once Patty understood her dilemma I could support her to either make a commitment or stop complaining.

Bill had been married for nearly two years when his wife, Judy, asked for a divorce. During their marriage, Bill had developed a strong and loving bond with Paul, Judy's five-year-old child from her first marriage. Despite the breakup, Bill wanted to maintain the relationship with his stepson. Judy was suspicious. She knew that Paul loved Bill, yet she sensed that Bill might use her son to extend his contact with her.

One afternoon, Bill took Paul skating and brought him home late. This angered Judy and precipitated a clash. She told him that he couldn't see Paul again. Bill lashed back, calling her unforgiving and selfish.

"What do you want?" I asked Bill after he explained his dilemma.

"My relationship with Paul has nothing to do with Judy. It's good for Paul and good for me. She knows that. She's being vindictive, taking her frustrations out on me and on Paul. I resent her interference with Paul's happiness. She knows I'm healthy for him."

"What do you want?" I asked again. This might be the most common question I ask my clients. I generally repeat it whenever an answer is not clear or a client seems stuck.

"I want to be able to see Paul and maintain our bond. I love that boy and he loves me." Bill was frightened that Judy might take his stepson away. She had that authority. His body tensed and shook as he recognized his helplessness.

"You want Judy not to interfere with you and Paul. That's clear. And if that's all you want, you could make it happen. But it seems to me you want something else."

"Well, I would like to work things out with Judy, if we could."

Here was the conflict. And where there's conflict there are competing desires. Bill wanted Paul *and* he wanted Judy. Five weeks before he had had both, and even though his marriage had been difficult, the comforts of the past seemed better than his present loneliness. But yesterday's options were no longer available. Judy was through. She had no desire to be with Bill again.

My job was to help Bill sort through his current options so he could prioritize them and make clear choices.

"You would love it if everything worked out with Judy," I continued. "I understand that. You also seem angry—furious even—that she quit, gave up on you and the marriage without giving it a fair chance."

"I *am* angry."

"What do you want from Judy?"

"I want a second chance."

"You want a second chance at the relationship and you want access to Paul. Anything else?"

"Sometimes I'd like to smash her in the face," Bill laughed, releasing some tension. "Not really. You know, she just drives me nuts sometimes."

"What does Judy want?"

"She wants me not to push myself on her. She keeps telling me she needs space."

"You want things that are in conflict. For Judy to allow you to be with Paul, she needs you to leave her alone. Your contact with Paul creates conflict with Judy. What do you want the most—Paul or Judy?"

"I want both."

"Right now you're getting neither."

"I know."

"What do you want?"

"I love Paul. I want to be able to see him—take him to the park or the movies, have him over for dinner. I relish our time together." Bill began crying. "This boy means so much to me."

"Can you do more to make sure this relationship works?"

"I guess I have to give up trying to get Judy back. But I want her also."

"Yes. You have to act and speak with a single intention instead of sending conflicting messages. If you don't want to lose Paul, you have to let Judy know that you won't use him to manipulate her. It only pushes her away. You can't fake this, Bill. She'll pick up your mixed signals instantly."

"You're right there," Bill nodded.

"Acting purely with Paul may even help you get back with Judy, but don't count on that. If she saw that your relationship with Paul didn't pull on her, she might start trusting you. If she feels like you're using him to get close to her, she'll feel manipulated and pull further away."

"She already has."

"Can you get her to trust you again?"

"If I apologized, that would help. I was late and that screwed up her afternoon a bit. I was supposed to drop him off without any contact, but because I was late I wanted to explain what happened."

"Was that a manipulation?"

"Might have been."

"Was it?" I pressed further.

"Yes."

"If you let her know that you've been in conflict, that you've been subtly manipulating the situation, and that you plan to cut it out and keep your relationship with Paul absolutely clean—how would she respond?"

"If I did that, she'd trust me again. I know she would. She would like Paul to have me in his life."

The session began with Bill blaming Judy for ruining his relationship with Paul. It turned around when Bill realized what he wanted and courageously accepted his part in the problem.

He started as a victim and left empowered because he prioritized his desires. He distinguished between his desire to stay in contact with Judy and the conflicting desire to spend time with Paul. Once he realized that his desires conflicted, he could face his pain and choose wisely.

In a larger sense, Bill's dilemma with Judy was indicative of the impasse that destroyed their marriage. Frequently their conversations ended in mutual frustration. Their typical fights concluded with Judy screaming, "You're not listening to me. I can't get through to you." She felt that Bill manipulated her with his subtle dishonesty. But Judy was unable to pinpoint her discomfort and to communicate her problem clearly. She knew something was wrong, but her vagueness left both partners troubled.

The question that could have broken the impasse, "What do you want?" was never asked clearly or persistently enough by either party. The fighting escalated out of control until, in desperation, Judy demanded a divorce.

The idea is simple, yet neglected. Find out what you want.

Would that I could implant a little microchip near your ear that activates each time you feel stress. In a soft, soothing tone it would say, over and over: "Find out what you want most. Get clear. Make a choice. Find out what you want most, get clear, make a choice. Find out what you want most, get clear, make a choice."

Confusion: A (Temporarily) Painless Solution

Bill had much to gain by staying confused. His friends took his side, sympathizing with the lousy way Judy treated him. And as long as he and Judy were fighting he felt some connection to her. Once Bill saw his dilemma and acted responsibly, feelings of rejection flooded him. The primacy of his sadness could no longer be avoided. The confusion, masked as secondary anger, had kept Bill from facing and ultimately accepting reality.

Confusion is so prevalent because it is inviting. It helps us avoid the harsh reality of choosing. But as I told Bill, "Right now you're getting nothing. Give up manipulating Judy and accept her decision and you can at least have Paul. Don't give her up and you'll lose both." It takes courage to know what we want and to act accordingly. We don't get hung up only on negative choices, sometimes even positive choices create problems. I want to play tennis, I want to write this book. I can't do both at the same time. My confusion lifts the moment I prioritize my desires and give one up. To do that I must check in with myself respectfully, ever aware of the need for balance in my life. Then I have to make up my mind and graciously let go.

Distinguishing Commitment and Desire

A commitment is different than a desire, which may be just a temporary feeling or strong urge. A commitment is a *stand*, based on an intrinsic faith we have in ourselves to know what is true and in our best interest. By holding certain truths to be self-evident, we build our lives around commitment. Commitment is the ultimate human power because it allows our love and our spirituality to develop and deepen. Our commitments define our identities and shape our actions. We are known to ourselves and to others by the commitments we make.

Commitment isn't based on logic or conventional rationality. Its source is more intuitive and mysterious. Its power can be recognized, cultivated, and channeled more easily than it can be defined. Commitments inspire in proportion to the price they exact. Gandhi's willingness to fast until the fighting stopped in India is an example of a commitment to peace.

Desires, on the other hand, are passing thoughts and hopes. They have little staying power and often conflict. Changing from moment to moment the way clouds sail haphazardly across the sky, desires come from nowhere and disappear back into the void. Defining myself by my desires leaves me in a perpetual state of confusion—blown around by each conflicting thought, never knowing where I stand or what truly matters. Desires determine what I eat for dinner. Commitment announces who I am as a human being.

Giving Up Illusory Commitments—Charlene

Charlene called to set up an initial appointment because she wanted to lose weight. "Have you tried the traditional weight loss places like *Weight Watchers* or *Overeaters Anonymous*?" I asked. Since my book, *Habit Breakthrough*, describes a process for breaking unwanted habits, many clients initially seek me out to help them shed pounds. Generally, I discourage such callers, directing them instead to local support groups. Psychotherapy is a tough, rigorous process requiring not only tenacity but a deep willingness for self-examination. Being overweight doesn't necessarily make someone a good candidate for therapy. Before I meet someone I like to give them a sense of what to expect.

"I'm not a weight loss counselor," I explained to Charlene over the phone. "I'm a psychotherapist who works with overweight people only after they've failed with other approaches." She seemed relieved to know that I would take a holistic look at her weight, and we set up an appointment.

After exchanging a few amenities, Charlene settled herself onto the couch and began speaking about her past. She had grown heavier as she grew older. In high school she was plump. In college, overweight. Now twenty-eight, she bordered on obese. Despite her extra weight, or perhaps because of it, she was meticulous about her appearance. Her color-coordinated outfit, complete with matching shoes and jewelry, as well as her neatly combed and immaculately layered short blond hair, spoke of a woman conscious about image.

After hearing about her past, I asked, "What's your goal? What would you like to accomplish here?"

The directness of my question seemed to embarrass her. She reached for the pillow on the sofa and held it for protection. Tentatively, she asked. "Do you mean how much weight do I want to lose?" A shy half-smile curled her mouth. She was almost too polite. Our conversation felt like the warm-up to a game.

I nodded. "That's a good place to start. How much would you like to weigh and how long do you think it should take to reduce?"

"Maybe a hundred pounds." Her cheerful demeanor evaporated as she talked about her weight. "I don't like to admit that I'm that heavy but I really am. I weigh more than 220 and I'm only 5'3". I hate being fat, and I hate admitting that I'm fat."

"How long do you think it will take to drop the 100 pounds?"

"A year or so?" Charlene wasn't prepared for such detail, yet I needed to understand her expectations.

"You say you want to lose weight. Is that the same as a commitment to lose weight?"

"I don't know. I know I want to lose weight," she said. "You want to," I said speaking softly, "but I'm not sure what that means. A college student may want to become a doctor. But getting an M.D. requires a commitment to years of study. Many desires have to be sacrificed to reach certain goals. Giving in to our desires can be temporarily gratifying, but in the long-run they can mess us up."

Charlene was listening attentively. She looked glad that I was talking and that the attention was off her. I continued, "Desires don't empower us. They don't necessarily make our lives better—in fact they make our lives worse when we waste time worrying about things we have no control over. Wanting the weather to be nice for tomorrow's picnic is an example. Since we don't control the weather, we're smarter when we don't think and hope about it."

"I often wish I could shut myself up," Charlene piped in. "My mind works overtime."

"You worry about losing weight?"

"All the time," she said.

"That worry does you no good. Unless your desires motivate and inspire you towards making and keeping commitments, I say get rid of them. Instead of thinking as you often do, 'I want to lose weight,' ask yourself the question, 'Am I committed to losing weight?'"

"That's the right question," Charlene agreed. But she looked pensive. After a long pause she said, "I don't know if I'm committed to losing weight."

"Just asking the question helps you understand that there's a difference between commitment and desire, doesn't it?" I was responding to the precious expression of discovery on Charlene's face. She had long told herself that she wanted to lose weight, just as almost everyone who smokes will tell you that they want to quit. But when she asked herself if she was committed to losing weight, the basic obstacles between her and a slimmer body came quickly to mind.

"Is commitment a feeling?" she wondered.

"I really feel like losing weight," I said. "Is that the same as being committed to losing weight?"

"It's not," she replied. "I see the difference."

At this point I reviewed some of the differences between desires and commitments. Her eyes told me she was beginning to grasp the distinction. When I sensed that she understood it intellectually, I challenged her to create a commitment.

"Suppose you say, just for the feel of it, 'I am committed to losing weight.'"

"You want me to *say*, 'I am committed to losing weight?'" She seemed taken aback.

"Words have power. Sometimes we don't know what's true or not true until we hear ourselves speak it. It's like trying on new clothes. You can't tell how well they'll fit until they're on your body. So try on this sentence: 'I am committed to losing weight.' Then tell me about your experience. This will help you get to know yourself better. Maybe you really aren't ready to lose weight, but maybe you are. This is a way of checking in with your more intuitive self."

Looking both intrigued and puzzled, Charlene said, "I think I understand what you're talking about, but whether I say 'want' or 'committed,' will it really make a difference?"

"Try it out. Simple words. I am committed to losing weight."

Charlene laughed nervously. "I don't know if I *am* committed to losing weight." She shrunk into the couch like a scared child as a tremor passed through her. "I can't say it. Just thinking those words scares me—shivers go up my spine."

"Are you sure that's fear?" I asked. "Maybe it's just some growing pains. This may be easier than you think. Try it: 'I am committed to losing weight.'"

"My body starts shaking when I even think of saying those words. I'm not committed to losing weight. I'm scared shitless about losing weight. That's the truth. I'm not ready." After a long pause she added, "Now I understand. There *is* a difference between wanting to lose weight and being committed. I can experience the difference."

"You want to lose weight," I said. "That's why you came to see me. But one thing at a time. Losing weight must not be the right first step. Suppose we just talk a while. I'd like to get to know you better."

That sounded great to Charlene. Our therapy would begin not with weight loss but with how she came to be so out of touch with her body. It was more than a year before we tackled the issue of weight directly.

The pivotal point in our conversation occurred as Charlene felt her body literally shake as she recognized the distinction between commitment and desire. At that moment, she gave up the illusion that she was ready to lose weight. She had been deluding and badgering herself by thinking she wanted to lose weight. To stop her crippling obesity from destroying her life, she needed to embark on a path that built her confidence and helped her make slow and steady positive changes. Before losing weight, Charlene had to gain confidence in her own integrity.

We often fail because we try to succeed at things we really aren't ready to succeed at. Picking our battles carefully is a crucial necessity. If a commitment to success can't be verbalized, then success is that much further away.

As Lao-tse said some 2500 years ago, "The journey of a thousand miles begins with one step." Goals have to be broken into finite pieces. The first step is to recognize when what we want and what we're committed to are different. Confusing the two spells trouble.

Transforming Desires into Commitments—Sarah

Sarah, a thin and fragile-looking thirty-two-year-old computer programmer, survived an unhappy childhood. Her dad was a withdrawn alcoholic who had little contact with the family. Her mother was a bitter woman who resented her husband's distance and ruled her daughter with an iron hand. Now and then the father exploded, breaking the quiet tension and terrifying his daughter. Sarah developed a docile, eager-to-please personality because she realized that a low profile meant less pain.

When Sarah was fourteen, her father began an alcoholic treatment program that helped him not only to quit drinking but also to stop his temper tantrums. Family life became more peaceful but Sarah carried many childhood wounds into her adult life.

Sarah's adult personal life was fraught with anxiety. Unable to be decisive and always fearful of offending anyone, she became a serious procrastinator. She also avoided close relationships with men. We both sensed that her difficulties traced back to unresolved childhood issues.

Sarah tried talking to her parents but she never pushed. Meaningful dialogues were avoided. If Sarah tentatively brought something up, her parents would retort: "We changed a long time ago—why can't you let go of the past?"

Sarah felt angry at and unsupported by her parents but afraid to say so. "When I get around them," she confessed, "I freeze up. I become that terrified little six-year-old girl caught in their warfare."

"That's the reason to confront them," I asserted. "You're not that kid anymore, even if you feel that way. There's no point in blaming them for the past, but you are entitled to tell them how you feel in the present. Speaking your peace will help you know that your childhood fears aren't still running you."

Sarah dreaded family visits. A few days before Christmas, she walked wearily into my office and put her hands over her face. Tears flowed. "My parents expect me for Christmas," she began. "I don't know what to do. I don't want to go. I don't know how to tell them. If I go, I wonder if I'll ever get out of this stupid docile role I play."

"Did you tell them you're coming?" I asked.

"They assume it. I always go back there for Christmas."

"What do you want?" I asked, getting to the point.

"I don't want to go. Working with you makes me realize something has to change. I don't want to spend Christmas with them."

"So why not tell them that?"

"Scared, that's why." Sarah put her head down and looked away. "I feel hopeless," she said. "I can't stand it."

I summarized her dilemma. "So the only way for you to feel good about yourself is either to not go at all or go and talk to them. The worst scenario would be to go and not talk and leave the status quo untouched."

"There's another piece," she added. "My friend Jennifer invited me to Christmas at her home. Frankly, that feels like the right thing to do."

"What did you tell her?"

"That I'd think about it. If I do that I'll have to tell my parents, and they will have to get that we have a problem."

"You've created quite a dilemma. It's going to hurt but something good will come from this."

"They'll be really hurt if I skip Christmas." She shook her head, "But I guess I *want* to hurt them." Looking at me mournfully, she said, "I'm pretty mixed up, eh?"

"You certainly have conflicting desires tugging in different directions. What are you going to do?"

"I don't know."

"Do you want me to help you decide?"

"Yes." At last a definitive statement. "I can't decide what to do. It's really awful." She looked nervously around my office, fidgeting first with her hair and then with a thin gold bracelet.

"Are you willing to reach a decision during our session?" I was looking for a commitment to clarity.

"I want to decide, I really do. Christmas is next week!" She sounded more desperate than resolved.

"Are you willing to make a decision during our time together?" I repeated. Her first response was unsatisfactory.

"I want to. I just told you."

"I didn't ask if you want to. I know you want to. I asked if you are willing to. Willing to means making a firm commitment, right now, about a course of action." I was friendly and respectful, but firm.

"I think so." She was stalling for time so I gave her a little.

"Do you have all the information you need to make the decision tonight?" I asked.

"I already know everything I need to know, if that's what you mean. Nothing's going to change."

"Great," I replied. "Are you willing to make the decision tonight during our conversation?"

"Boy, you push hard. This is very painful. I really want to make up my mind—the sooner the better."

"Sarah, your habit is to keep yourself on the hook so you don't have to risk more pain. If you really want to make up your mind then you'll shift that desire into a commitment, let the wave of energy or fear pass through you, and accept that risk is part of the commitment process. Desire and commitment are not the same."

"This scares me."

"I'm scared of a lot of things, too. Commitment scares everyone. But don't let that stop you. You have to be willing to act even if your heart is pounding and your palms are sweating."

Sarah was cornered. I said nothing and waited in silence for over a minute. To Sarah, it must have felt longer. Then she stood up suddenly, walked nervously to the window and sat down. She didn't know what to do with herself. Next she sighed loudly several times. Finally she nodded her head. "I can't keep procrastinating. Yes, I will make up my mind during this session." She paused with great relief and asked, "Now what?"

"Good," I said. "You're on the right track. Let's do a little process that helps you check in with what's really right for you. I'll say two different sentences and then ask you to repeat them.

Pay attention to your reaction. After taking her through a brief relaxation process, I said, "I am going to spend Christmas at my parent's house." Then after a long pause, "I am going to spend Christmas with Jennifer." After Sarah repeated each sentence she looked at me and said, "The first sentence made me tense, the second one relaxed me."

If we were salespeople, the next section of our interaction would be called, "The close." The customer has been admiring the goods long enough. The time has come to commit. Salespeople know this is the moment that counts. Sarah's experience would be for naught unless she rephrased her experience using the language of commitment to create a clear course of action. "So is it settled? Are you clear what you're going to do?"

Suddenly Sarah tightened up, squirming in her chair.

"I don't know why this is so hard. I know what I need to say. It's just so hard."

"You'll get better with practice," I added encouragingly. "As you get into a new groove of speaking your commitments clearly, you'll see how much easier life becomes."

"All right. I'm going to Jennifer's home for Christmas. I'm going to call my parents and let them know. They'll be upset. And who knows, maybe this will break the ice and we'll start talking."

"When are you going to let them know this?" I was checking that the decision was hers and that it was grounded in reality.

"Tonight. I'll call them as soon as I get home."

"Well done, Sarah!" I was impressed with her sudden decisiveness.

In the months that followed, the ice broke between her and her parents. Staying away at Christmas gave a message they couldn't ignore and precipitated some healing dialogue.

By transforming her desire into a commitment, Sarah was able to clarify her struggle so she could face her fears and choose decisively. Commitment is distinguished from desire by the way we speak about it. Our bodies carry an intuitive awareness of this distinction. Sarah stiffened the moment I asked for a commitment. If such a distinction didn't exist, her body would not have reacted spontaneously and fearfully to my question, "Are you willing to make up your mind?" The possibility for clarity always exists, but we must choose it. Our process reminded her of this untapped power to choose.

Before we can listen clearly we must speak clearly. Before we can speak clearly we must know what we want. Understanding what we want requires elevating certain desires into commitments while dropping the others. If life were a simple logical experience, this would be easy. The addition of intense emotional attachments makes the process difficult but not impossible.

From Desire to Commitment: The Steps

The process of dispelling confusion by first getting clear about what you want and then elevating certain desires into commitments sounds simple: You make up your mind, state your commitments, and then follow through. In a world full of thousands of shifting variables, this is easier said than done.

This section walks through three basic steps that help us create and then honor commitments. There's also a contingency plan if troubles persist. Step one requires that we isolate and acknowledge the problem. Step two asks us to state the commitment clearly. Step three checks if the commitment is realistic.

Step 1: Isolate and Acknowledge the Problem

Common sense tells us that we can't solve a problem before we recognize it. The first hindrance to commitment-making is our tendency to avoid facing difficult situations. People get lung cancer or heart disease before they quit smoking or change their diets. The price is often not seen until too late. Sometimes we become complacent with or resigned to a situation that can be changed. Until we declare something unacceptable, it isn't.

When I first became a single parent, mornings were unpleasant. Instead of starting with a sweet, gentle routine, the day was hectic and irritating from the moment the alarm blared noisily until after the kids were hustled out the door—late for their bus. We hassled about everything: what to eat for breakfast, what to pack for lunch, what to wear to school, and what the afternoon plans required. Mornings were tolerated, not appreciated. So it had been when I was a kid, and I assumed that this was how all families operate. Although tense and uncomfortable, I never isolated the mornings as a particular problem. Just as rain gets you wet, I figured, mornings are tense.

Then one day the irritation reached a critical mass. Fed up, I vowed to do things differently. Talking it over with my kids, we devised several changes: getting up earlier, going over lunch menus in advance, laying out clothes. Within three weeks, we had established healthy new patterns. The problem seemed so easy to solve that I felt like a jerk for not realizing it sooner. Acknowledging a problem is step one for change.

When I meet a new client, one of my first tasks is to scan different issues and separate them into manageable chunks. Although all problems relate to our personality and to the basic values by which we live, still it's essential to isolate problems so we can tackle and address them one at a time.

Step 2: Know Your Expectations

Once we've isolated and acknowledged the problem, we need to know what we expect from ourselves. Unclear expectations cost us dearly. They can even dampen our sex lives.

John and Annie were two delightful folks in their early thirties who came to therapy for what might be described as a tune-up. John was tall and thin. Soft, curly black hair highlighted his kind, soft eyes. He seemed earthy and available. Annie, too, was easy to like. Her innocent, youthful smile emanated friendliness. I quickly saw why John had fallen in love with her.

Their marriage was strong, they said. But before starting a

family, they wanted to discuss a key issue that was troubling them—sex. Both had good jobs and plenty of love and goodwill towards each other, but after being together for eight years their sex life was sagging.

John began. "She isn't as turned on by me as she once was and it worries us."

As with nearly everyone else brought up in our sexually biased culture, certain stereotypical gender roles had been imprinted on them. Annie was cast as the caregiver and John the provider. Although their income levels were even and they worked to avoid problems, something was out of balance. It was common for Annie to place John's needs before hers. She said with a little irritation, "You get your way much more than I do." John shrugged in acknowledgment, "I guess I do."

"With all things," I asked, "or just in sexual power struggles?"

"When it comes to wanting sex, that's when he gets his way," Annie clarified. John looked uncomfortable and gazed vacantly out the window. Suddenly he caught himself withdrawing and sat closer to Annie as if to remind himself to not become defensive. He was here to change.

"Do you have an agreement or clear expectation that you make love only when both of you feel like it?" I asked.

"Of course," Annie replied almost automatically. But after thinking about it, she clarified: "Sometimes John seems needy so I do it more out of obligation than from lust or desire. Plus he pouts if I don't want to." John winced.

"So it's not like you've ever needed an agreement, because it's understood that love-making is voluntary? Most couples don't need to talk about this stuff at the beginning of a relationship. But that makes it harder to talk about now because it's never been talked about before."

"I guess I don't like to make love as often as he does and it confuses me," Annie said. "I think I should."

"But it wasn't always that way?"

"Right. I don't know when I stopped feeling so sexual. It's been a gradual decline," she said.

As we talked, I learned that the couple's sexuality was based increasingly on John's biological urges. Annie would make love not because of passion but because her husband was insistent and she wanted to please him. At times her sexual pleasure was tentative. Sometimes she felt like it, but often she was bored and hoped John would finish his business quickly. John grew frustrated when he sensed his wife was not enjoying him. Their once-heated passion was becoming lukewarm.

As we probed, an old pattern surfaced. One of Annie's previous relationships had been undermined because her lover was dissatisfied with her mild sexual appetite. She had angrily left him, but the hurt had never left. She had been embarrassed to talk to John about this relationship. But she was scared that her lack of passion could ruin her marriage. Instead of paying careful attention to her body, trusting that her natural sexual appetite was sufficient, she felt obligated to please her man whenever he expressed a strong desire.

John's pouting when he didn't get his way took unconscious advantage of his wife's fears. Annie's extra guilt further threw off her rhythm and triggered an even greater decline in her amorous desires. John felt the distance and became needier. Their original, unstated agreement to make love only by mutual consent was being lost in a swirl of confusing feelings.

Annie was angry. In trying to please her husband, she had also minimized the role biology played in the cyclical nature of her sexual desire, further pushing her out of touch with herself. Helping her get in touch with and express her anger immediately freed up her energy.

John's pouting revealed a certain sadness that carried over from a childhood in which he often felt neglected. As the couple explored their feelings more, they were able to clarify their expectations.

Much as a wife might like to please her husband or vice versa, no marriage can sustain itself if the partners don't take responsibility for their own well-being. Solid relationships require solid individuals. When Annie's desire to please her husband took precedence over her commitment to her own well-being and to the unspoken agreement to make love voluntarily, a breakdown occurred. She no longer was clear about what she expected from either herself or her husband. The balance between giving and receiving was thrown off and her sexuality suffered as a result.

"What's needed?" I asked.

Annie spoke first. "I need to know John isn't going anywhere just because we're working through this. When Gene slept with other women, I felt destroyed. I thought I was past that, but as we talked about all of this I feel those old fears again."

"I'm not going to let a little glitch in our sex life ruin our marriage," John said emphatically, reaching out and taking his wife's hand.

"How about a big glitch?" Annie wanted additional reassurance.

"I'm committed to you. We'll work it out. This is as much my problem as yours. I'm the one who is always pulling at you. Maybe something is wrong with me."

"I do need you to stop pressing me. I feel oppressed by you sometimes. It makes it harder to be naturally affectionate. If you were less insistent I could get into it, but your neediness pushes me away."

"I don't want to be a sexual charity case. I want the passion back that we used to share." I sensed that John was trying to resolve his own confusion. A healthy dialogue was opening up.

The process of talking this through—calmly and lovingly—went a long way towards rekindling this couple's sexual energy. They each had to take a step back and examine their expectations before they could move forward. Many couples know their relationship is getting worse but are afraid to do the work. Just as the strings of a musical instrument invariably need to be tuned, so we all need tune-ups. Being explicit about what we expect from others and ourselves reduces our confusion, making it that much easier to make and keep commitments.

Step 3: Make Commitments Realistic

A promise is a type of commitment in which we pledge to perform specific tasks by a designated time. It is precise. It clarifies expectations. It takes desires and elevates them not only into commitments but into specific expectations. A promise cuts through excessive verbiage and reveals the core issues. In a story told earlier, Sarah broke through old patterns and fears when she promised to make a decision by the session's end. Likewise, Sally's breakthrough occurred when she promised to live for the next six months.

When we promise to break old patterns we put ourselves at risk. I once promised my son Hilly that I would not raise my voice around him for a week. Four days later, when he was being particularly aggravating and I started getting louder, he said, "Gee, Dad, you promised not to yell at me. Don't you think it's important to keep your word?" That shut me up. Having a clear expectation made it easier to break an unwanted habit. I empowered my kid to support me and we both ended up winning.

Speaking with clarity and precision about commitment makes it easier to keep our word. When we know what we're promising, we work harder to achieve it. Still, not all commitments can be kept. In our rush towards the good life our dreams, hopes, and desires often overshoot a realistic appraisal of our strengths and weaknesses: We end up promising beyond our ability to deliver. In baseball, batting average is a key statistic. Even a small difference can mean millions of dollars to a player. In the realm of keeping our promises, our average is also crucial. No one is perfect. But our trust goes to those who are more consistently trustworthy. The quickest way to have life fall apart is to fail to keep a good percentage of our promises.

But making only *safe* promises and keeping them all is no ticket to success. Powerful people make powerful promises and keep most of them. To use the commitment-making process as a vehicle for growth we need to stretch—not too much and not too little.

To stay balanced as the tightrope is raised to more impressive heights, we must keep making new commitments even as we learn from our failures . It's a scary process because there's no safety net. A crash can kill or maim us. Yet without risk, we fall asleep.

Earlier I talked about Rick, who felt like he was losing his mind when he tried to quit smoking before he was ready. His commitment was unrealistic; yet he needed to make it and fail, so that he could be humbled enough to look at his pain, integrate it, and move on.

Learning to speak the language of commitment and to communicate impeccably with others are skills that can be achieved with hard work. Making realistic commitments and using them to grow and expand is more difficult. It requires a willingness not only to play hard but also to examine our failures compassionately and rigorously and learn from them. As we grow and are humbled by life, we slowly discover the art of biting off only what we can chew.

One of my most painful experiences was the failure of my marriage to Lindy. In retrospect, our promise to love, honor, and cherish one another in sickness and in health, for better or for worse, until death do us part, was an unrealistic one that neither of us could keep. I tell the story with hope that it will shed some light on this most difficult aspect of the commitment-making process.

We met when I was twenty-five. I had already graduated from college, taught two years of elementary school in New York

City, traveled through much of the world, and lived for several years in a remote Mayan village in Guatemala. I had suffered and loved through several serious relationships, buried my mother, been to jail in Guatemala when a peasant set fire to my house (guilty in that culture until proven innocent), and studied with a guru. I was ready to settle down, have children, and find a career.

Lindy, on the other hand, was only twenty. She was blessed with an enormous capacity to love but had considerably fewer life experiences. We came from different backgrounds. I was blind to our differences.

She was in no rush to have children, settle down, or domesticate her adventurous spirit. I wanted kids and easily convinced her to comply. In retrospect I believe her decision was based in large part on a fear of losing me. Our first son, Peter, was conceived less than six months after we met. Love conquers all, we foolishly thought.

Lindy and I expected to be married forever. We hoped that our love would blossom and include whatever new interests we developed. And for most of the first eight years this happened. We literally built a home together, brought up two energetic and delightful boys, and shared friends and interests. We supported each other financially as, in turn, we each went back for more schooling. Our marital commitment helped us face conflicts and resolve difficulties.

Then things changed. At the end of a restful week-long Mexican vacation, I was ready to go home and resume our life. I loved my new job and, after years of living in many different places, was happy to be settled. When Lindy said she could easily spend another six months in Mexico, I knew trouble was brewing. She felt like her vacation had barely begun. I was shocked by how differently we saw things. She wanted to travel and play and find excitement. I looked forward to getting back to work.

After finishing graduate school, I wanted to use our savings as a down payment on a house. The idea bored her. "Let's use the money to travel to Asia—take the kids out of school for a few years. Let them get a different education. A house," she reasoned, "may be important but it could come later." I understood how she felt, since at one time I had quit my teaching job, packed all my worldly goods into a knapsack, and taken off to see the world. But I had done that already. I respected her needs, but mine were different.

I was scared. Our paths were changing. Differences we could not have foreseen when we made our lifetime commitment were erupting. Either of us could have saved the marriage by giving in to the other's goals. But we weren't willing. For more than a year we struggled to find suitable compromises. We had hit a terrible impasse.

A year after our vacation, Lindy left the marriage for a life of adventure. Within months she met a professional wind surfer whose livelihood required that he follow the wind. As her passport filled with exotic stamps, I bought a home and settled down. Eighteen months later, after my grief subsided, I met and later married Kathy, another psychotherapist with goals similar to my own.

For Lindy and me, love was not enough. After the initial feelings of betrayal passed, we realized that and had a no-fault divorce. Incompatible goals mean an incompatible relationship. Even the enormous devotion that we shared for our boys couldn't justify living unhappily. Children, after all, need healthy, fulfilled parents.

Looking back I wondered whether my original marital commitment was unwise or unrealistic. Although it worked for eight years, it was intended for life. The eighteen months preceding the separation were awful. Lindy's vitality dried up, and a massive confusion strangled her spirit. Being married wasn't working. But what about our lifelong commitment? How could she justify walking out on a decent husband and a wonderful family? As the initiator of the divorce, Lindy felt a crushing guilt that took years to subside. Yet she needed more than I could provide. She stayed longer than she should have because of our commitment. Finally she felt so dead both spiritually and emotionally that she realized she had to leave. Was our path made more difficult because of our original wedding vows? Could we have created a more realistic commitment?

This story is sad, disturbing, and decidedly unromantic. We did not live happily ever after. We did not compromise or work out our differences. Yet there's no villain and no hero. Just two caring human beings with different goals who married too young and whose "mistakes" brought great pain and two beautiful children. Now that we don't live together, our commitment towards the children helps us maintain a satisfying friendship. But friendship was not our original intention.

There could be other valid ways to interpret our divorce. Other factors obviously also played a part. The reasons for divorce are complex. But one aspect of the failure was the nature of our commitment in the first place. Would a more realistic commitment have lessened our trauma? Would that have made it easier for us to separate when the time came? Would it have made me less angry when I perceived her needs to be different? Would it have taken pressure off us and maybe even helped us work things out?

In retrospect I don't think our wedding vows served us. They weren't realistic and didn't help guide us through hard times. Neither of us knew ourselves or each other well enough to promise a lifetime. Yet we made the promise anyway.

In sharp contrast, before Kathy and I married, we wondered out loud if we had learned enough from our previous failures to not make the same mistakes. We used our wedding vows to fashion a commitment that still helps us stay present to our struggles. We promised each other honesty and a commitment to giving one another the benefit of the doubt. We also promised to support each other in our respective commitments. There was no talk of time limits, but rather of quality in the moment. Our faith is that each of us is committed enough to our individual growth to gain inspiration from the other.

Knowing my past should make it easy to understand why I was somewhat restrained when two of my clients bounced into my office one sunny afternoon and said, "Congratulate us, Mitch. We're getting married." Bob and Denise had worked in therapy for close to a year to strengthen their relationship. I respected their hard work. Their sessions were tough and productive and I watched with pleasure as their bond deepened in their daily life.

"That's great," I said with genuine enthusiasm as they snuggled into the sofa together. They acknowledged me for helping them and I, in turn, affirmed their readiness for marriage. Then I asked a strange and disconcerting question. "How long do you plan to stay married?"

After a long silence, Bob tentatively said, "We expect for life." Denise nodded her agreement and added, "We hope forever."

"I hope so, too, but will hope keep your commitment flourishing? What if you go through major changes? What if he turns into a jerk?" I asked Denise. "Or suppose she becomes irrational and angry, always finding fault with you, Bob. Suppose one of you becomes infatuated with someone else? Will you be there twenty years from now no matter what?"

They shrugged and stayed quiet. I was throwing a nasty curve to test their commitment. Better to be tested now, I figured, than later. I wanted them to think deeply about their relationship.

"How long can you promise to be together and know that, no matter what, you will honor your commitment to the marriage?"

Bob looked confused. "Is that a fair question?"

"I'm not sure," I said honestly. "We can drop the matter if

you like. Love feels like forever, but romance and reality sometimes collide. Maybe working with the question will help you clarify your commitment."

After a long silence, Bob turned to face Denise. He spoke slowly, trying to feel the words as he said them. "I'm not planning to ever leave you. I love you. Look how much we've been through and worked out. I feel we have the tools to handle anything that comes up. Anything. But even if things got terrible, if we hit some irreconcilable differences, I'd give it five years of fighting before I quit. I would bet my life that we'll be married for at least five years." He stayed quiet for a while, thinking about what she said. Then he added, "On some level that feels right."

I watched closely. I was impressed that the couple even fielded the question. They could have side-stepped the confrontation and I wouldn't have pressed the issue.

"Forever scared me," Denise confessed. "We talked about this once before, and it made us uncomfortable so we dropped the conversation. How can I know now what life will be like in fifteen years or thirty? But five years sounds real. I can promise to stay in this relationship giving it everything I've got for five years." Reaching for tissues and choking back her tears, she looked into Bob's eyes and said, "I don't like this five-year stuff—it seems weird. But I don't know, with divorce rates so high, it's pretty scary. Five years—I can live with that. In fact maybe I even like it. But I want you to know I'm not looking for an out. I want our love to grow forever."

After a long pause, I broke the intensity with some good-natured advice. "You might not want to tell too many folks about this." I wouldn't have understood it myself a few years ago. This is a conversation I save for couples who understand that it's never wise to make a commitment of this magnitude until you know yourself well enough to know you can keep it."

That conversation took place more than ten years ago. Two years after the five-year point, Denise and Bob hit tough times.

There was an affair, a separation, and then a reconciliation two years later. But they worked through their issues and felt secure enough to start a family. Before deciding to have kids they renewed their wedding vows, only this time they dropped their five-year plan. I don't know what would have happened without their five-year commitment. At the time it helped them frame their lives and be more honest with each other. Asking ourselves tough questions and examining our limits and expectations is always useful. Discovering when a commitment is realistic and appropriate is no easy task. Sometimes all we can do is ask the right questions.

A Contingency Plan: Fake It Till You Make It

A dear friend has been sitting with a Zen master at intensive meditation retreats for more than seventeen years. Last year, when the master was almost ninety, my friend sensed that he might be attending his last retreat. On the last day as he sat and listened to the master talk, tears were running down his face in gratitude for all that Roshi has provided him through the years. "Never had his words seemed so clear and so powerful," my friend told me. "Never before did I get so much from them."

"What did he say," I asked.

My friend paused a long time, reflecting on what might be this Zen master's final instructions. "I guess you could say it this way, though of course he didn't use these words: 'Fake it till you make it.' It's about intention." My friend goes to his Zen retreat, sits upright, unmoving, and practices being the Buddha. His thoughts may be crazy, the mosquito biting him may drive him to distraction: but he sits, breathing, practicing a path that he believes in. His devotion to his practice and his teacher uplifts him.

It takes faith to "fake it." If we aspire to be Christ-like and act that way, in time we will start feeling it and believing more in ourselves. The purity of our intentions becomes our greatest offering.

As a parent, I sometimes have to "fake" being loving. If I don't feel like getting up with a sick child at three in the morning, I can hide my dismay and "fake" graciousness. My intention is to be a loving parent. If I can't feel it, I can at least act the part. As we practice being gracious, authentic graciousness gradually arises, evoked by our intentionality.

When we're facing difficult choices and dilemmas, sometimes there's so much confusion and fear that we become immobilized. Rather than risk one choice or another, we freeze. At such times, we have to fake being powerful and decisive because doing so keeps us moving. Sometimes we have to "guess" a commitment to move things along. Guessing here means turning a hunch or an inclination into a short-term commitment. If nothing else, this process breaks up the ice. The worst that will happen is that our "guessed" commitment turns out to be unrealistic, unachievable, or simply not in our best interest. At that point we admit the mistake and revoke the commitment.

As important as it is to honor our word, it's worse to sit back indecisively and never take chances. That's why the revocation process can work if it is used only sparingly. I don't know any perfect people who keep their word a hundred percent of the time. We're human.

Guessing breaks the impasse, so guess and try your best to keep your word. If you fail, at least you've made a good-faith effort. In the best case scenario, the new commitment blossoms and flourishes. In either case, a new commitment is created and brings some risk.

When Jackie was driving herself nuts with confusion, I asked her to "guess" a commitment. Her relationship with Roger had started with a blaze of romance and glorious sexuality. At the outset their relationship looked like a match made in computer-dating heaven. They were hard-working, good-looking, sensitive young adults who both desired a long-term relationship. They had similar interests, goals, and education. Their affection was genuine. But it peaked after a few months. Something was missing. Jackie began to feel attracted to other men and occasionally pursued these feelings. Yet she kept returning to Roger.

Roger was ready for a commitment. Jackie hesitated. "I'm so confused," she admitted. "I can't decide what's best. Sometimes I think he's the man for me. Other times I find him boring and unappealing." Just as someone wearing blue sunglasses sees the world with a blue tint, Jackie's confusion and indecisiveness colored everything.

I suggested a short-term commitment. "Go full out for a few months. If things get better, you'll renew the commitment. If they get worse, at least you tried." She liked the idea but wanted to hear more.

"Pretend he's the last available man on the face of the earth. Your job is to enjoy him, make him right, fall in love. If you can't make it work with him, assume you're out of luck and are destined to a life of loneliness. Forget about tomorrow, forget your worries, and turn him into Prince Charming. Accept him as he is, and he'll relax and be even better. You both agree that your commitment expires at the end of three months, but don't think about that now. Do no evaluation until the three-month period is up."

Jackie looked intrigued. "But I don't know if I should do this."

"Guess it! Don't hold back. It's a short-term commitment. But the key word is commitment, not short-term."

"Guess it?" she repeated.

"You're stuck now. What do you have to lose?"

A big smile of relief slowly spread over her face. "It's okay to guess?"

"Yes, but don't make this commitment to find out what you

want. Make it because you have a genuine intention to love and enjoy Roger. Are you ready for this relationship to become wonderful?" I asked.

"I don't know," she honestly admitted.

"You've been saying that for months. You'll never find out if you don't stop vacillating. Fake it, maybe you'll make it."

The idea cut through Jackie's confusion. She told Roger that evening that she wanted a monogamous relationship and that she was going to stop her indecisiveness. She committed herself to no flirting, no fantasies about other men, and a genuine good-faith effort at resolving problems for the next three months. Roger loved it.

Jackie convinced everyone but herself.

Two days later, in an obvious crisis, she called in desperation. When she plopped onto the chair, she said with a flourish, "The crisis is over. A few hours after I made that commitment to Roger, I *knew* it was wrong."

"How did you know?"

"I walked out of here skeptical but optimistic. Then I told Roger. But instead of feeling good about it, I felt trapped. Okay. I ignored that feeling—tried to put those negative thoughts out of my mind. I couldn't, though. After I got home, my body started shaking—literally shaking—and I began to sob. I feel affection for Roger, but who am I kidding? I was crying because it was over. I wanted to call him to say good-bye. Next thing I know I call a different man I've been a little interested in and we take a nice long walk. If this commitment was right, my world wouldn't have collapsed so quickly. It's been hell, Mitch. I've got to believe that Roger isn't the man for me. The commitment woke me up, even if I did have to break it to get clear."

Jackie broke through the inertia of a confusing relationship the hard way. Sometimes that's the only way to do it. After several wishy-washy months with Roger, she used the power of commitment to find out where she stood.

I once found myself in a dilemma similar to Jackie's. I had been dating Kathy for eight or nine months. As we became closer, some hidden fears about women—tracing back to the break-up of my marriage with Lindy—began surfacing. Kathy was experiencing similar problems that stemmed from the ending of her previous relationship. We had both expected those earlier relationships to be for life. Sometimes we got stuck clinging to old memories, and that started us getting on each other's nerves for the first time. Lingering on yesterday dulled the luster of our new romance. We needed a booster shot, but neither of us felt like supplying it.

Fortunately, I remembered my own words to many procrastinating or fearful clients: "Fake it till you make it. Guess a commitment and take that risk."

Unilaterally, I made a six-month commitment. I asked of myself what I had asked of Jackie. Almost immediately my irritation faded. The relationship with Kathy began to soar.

Create a commitment. The feelings will follow. For Jackie, it brought an onslaught of raw emotion that pointed her in a new direction. For me, the commitment paved the way for marriage. In both cases clarity followed.

Powerful people, people who live full rich lives, make powerful commitments and keep them. But powerful people are also honest, respectful, and responsible with their imperfections. When their commitments fail or hit road blocks, as some inevitably will, they learn and keep growing. The quality of our lives is determined by the quality of our commitments. Playing full-out wakes us up. We can do no more.

6

The Art of Balance

H ONESTY, respect, responsibility, and commitment can be learned—given enough time and attention. But to apply these values with wisdom and flexibility we need balance. Commitment, for example, brings meaning to our lives; but if we over-commit, we can run ourselves ragged. Responsibility is the ticket to freedom; but if we're unbalanced, it quickly becomes a burden. When honesty is untempered by balance, we can be perceived as thoughtless and undiplomatic. In all things, balance is needed. Even our need for balance must itself be balanced. As the saying goes, "Everything in moderation, including moderation."

Balance isn't so easily learned. It follows no strict formulas and can't be obtained by reading books or adhering to specific rules. It takes grace and courage in the midst of living to find and appreciate balance. As we understand the necessity for balance, and start thinking about it more profoundly, our ability to tune into ourselves increases.

Balance requires intuition—an inner sense of knowing. You can't explain to a child how to ride a bike. You have to run and sweat and wait until the kid gets the feel for it. If the child brings courage and perseverance, then success will come sooner or later.

This kind of intuition takes time to develop and should not be confused with cravings and feelings. Your desire for a new car may be intense, and you may hear that car calling; but later, when you can't make the payments, you'll hear the bank calling. Discerning the difference between intuitive knowledge and an impatient or nagging desire requires wisdom. We have to slow down and develop a balanced relationship with ourselves.

To live in balance means to live on the tightrope; to embrace and accept the presence of risk as something that wakes us up and helps us be fully alive. Leonard Cohen, the poet and songwriter, once described a saint this way:

It is a kind of balance that is his glory. He rides the drifts like an escaped ski. His course is a caress of the hill. . . . Something in him so loves the world that he gives himself to the laws of gravity and chance.

Ultimately, achieving balance means making peace with the essential duality of all nature. As we learn to balance birth with death, sadness with joy, fear with peace, and pain with pleasure, then a blessed state gradually arises, and we can "caress" our way through life.

The amount of dullness or boredom in our lives shows how far our sense of caution is out of balance with our sense of adventure. As we grow older, we often tend to become creatures of fear and habit. We may drift toward staid, settled, and essentially boring lives. Henry David Thoreau reminds us that most people "live lives of quiet desperation." And Kahlil Gibran warns us that "the lust for comfort murders the passion of the soul, and then walks grinning in the funeral."

Minimizing risk stifles our passion for life. A bird in the hand isn't always worth two in the bush. Playing it safe can be a prescription for mediocrity. To bring passion to our lives, we sometimes need to trade in what we know for the unknown.

Balance requires clear thinking, self-discipline, a deep knowledge of our feelings, and an ability to keep a perspective. This requires great subtlety. The crux of the problem is that the subtle art and discipline of balancing can't always hold its own in the face of our not-so-subtle intense cravings and desires.

Balance and Discipline

Imbalance begins early because children are biologically programmed to seek the positive and avoid the negative. As we grow older, this tendency creates more and more problems. Growth requires a courageous willingness to face and work through difficulties. Finding balance in the way we discipline ourselves may be the toughest of all our challenges.

Most of us are too hard on ourselves when we fail. We don't know how to learn from our mistakes without punishing ourselves unduly. Self-discipline becomes balanced when we figure out how to get the job well done with the least amount of pain. For example, if I want to lose weight, I'll need a program of good nutrition and exercise that offers a gradual change from my present lifestyle. If I tackle something too radical or strenuous, it's likely to backfire and engender resistance—I've been too tough on myself. But, if the regimen isn't difficult enough, there won't be any positive long-term effect. In that case, I'm not tough enough. Starting out with a strong resistance to pain makes it difficult to find the balance between being simultaneously encouraging and nurturing, on the one hand, and tough and rigorous on the other.

Training ourselves and our children to live in balance requires an acceptance and appreciation of life's subtleties. I once heard emotional maturity defined as the ability to be in two different psychological mind-sets or spaces simultaneously. For example, can I chastise myself for going off my diet and also forgive myself for overeating? Perfect balance might require that I accept that I am simultaneously doing the best I can and not doing the best I can. Evaluating my behavior from that vantage point, I can then either put pressure on myself to perform better or relax and accept that I have done the best I can.

Just as a donkey can be motivated to move with both a carrot and a stick, we have to learn to motivate ourselves by balancing opposite poles. If I have to accept a tough failure or major loss, for example, my pain is softened if I can bring mercy and compassion along. But if the failure is a result of my laziness or poor judgment, I also have to correct those short-comings so they don't plague me in the future. The six most profound words in the English language may be "I love you," and "Cut the crap." Those six words are reduced to two in the catch-phrase "tough love." Without balance, neither the toughness or the love is enough.

Before making a big decision, we can ask a central question that helps us find our balance point: "Can I live graciously with the results and not engage in second-guessing?" Before acting, wait until you can promise yourself to be gracious even with fail-ure. This promise helps break the pattern of self-blame. Slowing down and asking this wonderful question makes it easier to acknowledge that balance and risk are part of life.

Balance and Fun

One summer afternoon when my oldest two children tried to teach me wind surfing, I learned a tough lesson in balance.

"Lean back," they yelled as I struggled to stand up on the wind-surfing board.

"If I lean back, I'll fall," I shouted.

"You may, but you may not."

I leaned back just a tad and the board slid forward ever so slowly.

"Dad, if you want to go faster and have some fun, you've got to lean back more and find your balance point. If you lean back too far, then next time you lean back a little less."

"I'll fall." I repeated lamely.

"It's water, Dad. You'll get wet. But when you get back on, you'll know where your leverage is best."

The problem was that I didn't want to fall. I had my contact lenses on and didn't want to risk losing them underwater. My children soon grew frustrated with my half-hearted attempts and gave up: "Dad, if you're not willing to fall, you can't learn to wind surf. So stop wasting our time."

To learn balance, we must take risks. We must experiment. The problem is that we don't think trial and error is fun. Yet when we were kids learning to walk, we were exuberant experimenters. Watch a little toddler. There's no self-condemnation, embarrassment, or shame about falling down twenty times in an hour. She just picks herself up and waddles on until she gets it.

As we get older we take the fun out of risk. No wonder we're out of balance. Ask for a volunteer in a kindergarten class and a roomful of children will eagerly throw up their hands, shouting and straining, "Me, me, me." Make the same request to a roomful of adults, and the squirming continues until someone reluctantly volunteers. Most of us feel that life is already tough enough, and we don't want additional risks.

Balance and flexibility are cut from the same cloth. To be effective we need extraordinary dexterity, for we never know what life will throw at us. In baseball, the term "soft hands" denotes an infielder's ability to stay alert to any unexpected hop that a wicked ground ball may take at the last second. If the fielder is too rigid in his position, he won't be able to adjust quickly enough to make the catch when the ball veers left or right. Our attitudes often serve as unyielding positions that make it difficult to achieve what we want.

The guidelines for balance and flexibility are the same. Practice, lighten up, pay attention to the big picture as well as the immediate one, and remember that whatever you do, sooner or later, life will get you. Angels fly because they take themselves lightly. Here are some stories that help reinforce these attributes.

A man I met at a party knew I was a therapist and was chatting with me about becoming a new father. Holding his precious five-week-old as we spoke, he asked, "Got any advice?" I paused and reflected on the great opportunity handed to me. Finally I said, "No matter what you do, you'll screw your kid up. It's hopeless, so enjoy him and relax." From our conversation I had sensed that, if anything, this man was too concerned with making mistakes and needed a nudge on the other side. If my impression had been that he was indifferent to the responsibilities of parenting, I would have offered advice that warned him of the dangers of messing up his child.

Coming home from work one day, I was greeted by my kid as he hung out of a tree limb about thirty feet in the air. "Hey Dad, look at me! It's great up here." Great for you, I thought uncomfortably. But what is a parent to do? If I order the kid down I'll instill a negative self-confidence that, if anything, will make him more likely to smash his head while tripping on a crack in the sidewalk. All I can do is go inside, relax, and have a little faith. This isn't an invitation or an excuse to ignore your child's dangerous behavior. Not all risky behavior is wise. But most of the time kids know best what their limitations are; our job as parents is to provide guidance when guidance is asked for, and then get out of the way to let our little ones experiment with their lives.

A marvelous story about the Dalai Lama illustrates how having fun lets us risk more joyfully and freely. His Holiness was in New York City to preside at a sacred Tibetan ritual before a huge throng in Madison Square Garden. A throne-like dais had been constructed, and upon it was a cluster of large pillows. Making a solemn entrance to preside at this holy ceremony, the Dalai Lama entered the arena with monks chanting and drums beating. He climbed up the steps to his seat, his robes trailing, and sat down upon the pillows. Then he noticed that his body bounced a bit on the pillows. Like a delighted child, completely unpretentious, he began bouncing, again and again. A joyful grin spread over his face and beguiled the thousands who were watching.

Imagine how most of us would react to the responsibility of conducting a sacred invocation before thousands of people. In the face of what to almost anyone else would have been a scary moment, the Dalai Lama was grinning and bouncing.

Experiment and have fun. Think balance.

7

The Intention of Love

WHILE watching a movie about a year ago, six-year-old Jake asked, "Why are there bad guys in the world?" Great question, I thought. But before I could open my mouth to tackle existential dilemma number one, Hilly, age eighteen, replied, "So we can appreciate the good guys. No bad, no good." The answer satisfied Jake completely. Knowing that his older brother wasn't thrown by such a question was probably more comforting to Jake than if his mother or I had answered.

Hilly's response gave a sense of peace and order to a chaotic universe. In eleven words he offered an answer to the existence of evil that was kind, appropriate, loving, and unpretentious. His reply was infused with a force that could be called intentional love.

Two conflicting energies fight within us. Christians label this a battle between good and evil, or God versus Satan. Buddhists frame the struggle differently, more in terms of being awake and mindful versus being asleep and ignorant. The Buddha's awakened presence vanquished the forces of illusion and ignorance. Regardless of the labels we use for these forces that pull on us, the energy we need to triumph is activated by an inner intention. Judeo/Christian prayer is one example of manifesting intentionality. Meditation practice likewise builds intentionality.

On a mundane level, it's commonly accepted that one needs willpower to break unhealthy habits. Will and intention are the same. They direct a powerful internal life-force that is ours to channel as we like—the source of our free will.

Will can be used to destroy or uplift. Hitler had enormous will; so does Mother Theresa. One negative aspect of will is stubbornness. That same energy working positively is called tenacity. A strong-willed child is tough to raise but, if the energy is channeled well, that child becomes well-equipped to take good care of him or herself.

Intention and will are words for the same force, but intention has more positive connotations. By joining love to intention, something emerges that exists exclusively to uplift and nurture. When we get stuck, if we can dip into ourselves and discover our intention to love, then we can find peace and solace regardless of the circumstance. When it comes down to it, we have to fight the forces of ignorance or evil with our intention to love.

Here are a few examples of how I have worked with intentionality.

Sheila was having anxiety attacks. Voices within her were screaming, among other things, "You are scum of the earth. You don't deserve a good life." These voices had grown stronger over the past few months, probably because several positive opportunities had arisen that threatened to shake up her status quo. She seemed afraid of success. She hadn't slept well in over a week and was having trouble concentrating at work.

First I helped her relax so she could understand the feelings and thoughts that she was fighting. The swirl of different emotions confused her. She soon identified rage and hatred. Then she also recognized how sad she felt. Her angry thoughts were the ones telling her she didn't deserve peace.

After a while, we also isolated part of her that had a genuine desire for healing. She hadn't previously identified her intention to love. She hadn't been treated lovingly as a child, and she barely recognized her hidden longing for comfort and solace. Her anxious voices had drowned out her calmer, more loving voices.

I asked her to repeat, over and over, that she wanted to heal, that she wanted to relax, that she wanted to stop hating herself. At first she resisted. "I don't deserve peace," she said. "I'm not worthy of love."

"That's your fear speaking," I gently and persistently informed her. "That's not the real you, even if it's the voice you're most familiar and comfortable with. You do deserve peace. Your parents said you were unworthy, but you don't have to believe that anymore. It isn't true." By the end of the session her anxiety was subsiding. She was contacting the part of herself that loves. She was allowing my intentional love to activate her own. As the weeks progressed she became better able to diffuse and ignore her anxiety. And anxiety ignored is no longer anxiety.

Paula, another client, was in the throes of a psychotic episode. She heard voices telling her she was supposed to die. During previous psychotic episodes she had tried to kill herself and several times came within a hair of success. Over and over I asked her to repeat that her intention was not to die. "Let God determine whether you are supposed to die," I said. "You stay out of it." She was not to cooperate with the voice of doom that told her death was near. Her fear was that she would act unconsciously, as she had in the past, and attempt to kill herself. "When we wake up our intention," I told her, "the harmful power of our subconscious fades." As she strove diligently to assert her intention to not hurt herself, she began calming down. In previous episodes she had never worked with anyone to consciously assert her intention. She got through this episode faster and with less medication than in the past, and with no self-destructive behavior.

Both Sheila and Paula wanted to heal. Their suffering was intense and they sought release. But the healing energy, which

I'm calling intentional love, was overpowered by the negative conditioning they had endured as children.

Sam had a session that illustrates how a child's craving for intimacy and love becomes distorted when parents act without loving intentionality. When Sam was fourteen, a gang of older teenaged thugs beat him up. He remembered lying on the street, desolate, physically bruised, and humiliated. He believed he had been an innocent victim. But when we drew out the details, he recalled that the older kids were walking on the other side of the street. It was Sam who started the fight by shouting some stupid epithet at them. Only after that did they cross the street, chase him down, and hurt him.

I helped him relive his trauma by role-playing the incident. I backed him into a corner, yelling in his face. This precipitated a memory that shook him to the core. "I started the fight because it felt comfortable to get beaten up. That's how my father related to me. He either ignored me or beat me up. I felt strangely comfortable—at home somehow. I felt it when you were yelling at me." For Sam to be hurt by others was not only normal, it was what he believed he deserved. In a distorted manner, it helped him feel closer to his father.

Sam wanted intimacy. Since his father had communicated violently, Sam linked violence to home and hearth. As he collapsed crying in my office, he realized with a new compassion for himself how his childhood wiring kept him repeating violent experiences. "All I really wanted was love," he told me. "Since my dad was angry all the time, I guess I thought that was love. No wonder I get into such messes."

Sam thought of himself as a tough guy: He wasn't a sensitive New Age type. He knew he had a violent side but hadn't realized that at its root, his self-destructive behavior was motivated by a desire for closeness with his father.

Shirley McClaine once said, "We get in life what we think we deserve." Sam thought he deserved violence. Sheila thought she deserved anxiety. Paula often thought she deserved death. But these beliefs and desires were not the original ones these clients were born with. These were views they adopted when faced with conflicting situations in childhood.

Gibran wrote:

> What is evil but good tortured by its own hunger and thirst?
>
> Verily, when good is hungry it seeks food even in dark caves, and when it thirsts it drinks even of dead waters. . . .
>
> In your longing for your giant self lies your goodness: and that longing is in all of you.

For Sam to heal he needed to contact his longing for his "giant self." He needed to realize that deep down his intention has been to love. Disguising our intention from others or ourselves is unnecessary. All we have ever wanted is love. And love is what we deserve. We have to go after it.

Forgiveness

One thing stops us from believing that we deserve to love and be loved. We don't forgive very easily—not ourselves, not others. This squashes our intention for love and perpetuates our suffering.

The Buddhist scripture quoted earlier bears reiteration. "Hatred never ceases by hatred. Only by love is hatred appeased." To uncover our intention to love, we must forgive. Forgiveness requires a recognition that we, too, screw up. It also requires that we have mercy for ourselves and compassion for others.

Forgiveness is the ultimate risk. At one point Sheila said, "I don't deserve to be healed. I've done many terrible things. If I forgive myself, how do I know I won't do those terrible things again and again?"

I told her that forgiveness is like money: You can't have too much of it. It's always useful and if you have any left over you can always give it away. She smiled. "But to believe that," I continued, "you must tune your intention to not hurt others and use your will for the good of humanity. And don't forget to include yourself as part of humanity."

To forgive we must trust that our intention is to heal. Like Sheila and Sam, we all long for peace. Even if we have done terrible things, punishing ourselves won't fix the problems. Hatred is never the answer.

Forgiveness and healing is the theme at the Vietnam Memorial where veterans, family members, and loved ones leave messages to those who have departed. One man left the following note, accompanied by a picture of a Vietnamese soldier with a little girl:

> Dear Sir,
>
> For twenty-two years I have carried your picture in my wallet. I was only eighteen years old that day that we faced one another on that trail in Chu Lai, Vietnam. Why you didn't take my life I'll never know. You stared at me for so long, armed with your AK-47, and yet you did not fire. Forgive me for taking your life, I was reacting just the way I was trained, to kill V.C. . . .
>
> So many times over the years I have stared at your picture and your daughter, I suspect. Each time my heart and guts would burn with the pain of guilt. I have two daughters myself now. . . .
>
> I perceive you as a brave soldier defending his homeland. Above all else, I can now respect the importance that life held for you. I suppose that is why I am able to be here today. . . .
>
> It is time for me to continue the life process and release my pain and guilt.
>
> Forgive me, Sir.

It was time for this soldier to put down his burden. Why we carry our burdens so long seems like one of life's ultimate mysteries. Some carry them for twenty-two days, some for twenty-two months, some twenty-two years, some forever. Carrying these burdens prevents us from being awake, from living with love, from accepting life exactly as it is.

To believe we deserve the best, we must work hard and we must work smart. This book has provided an overview of how to do that. Psychological and spiritual growth occurs when we couple insight with action. Since each courageous act brings forth more insight, a positive spiral of growth deepens. As we embrace the basic values of honesty, respect, and responsibility, it becomes easier to expand our insights and act courageously.

Honesty begins the process. As Shakespeare said, "To thine own self be true." Because rigorous honesty with ourselves and towards others takes courage, it expands our self-worth and helps us to believe we are deserving. Similarly, acting with respect requires a constant mindfulness. Unkind, disrespectful utterances and actions—like dishonesty—only undermine us, diminishing our energy of intentional love. As we deepen honesty and respect we take greater responsibility for how our lives are created and lived. Taken together we create a critical mass of good will or intentionality that allows us to live gracefully in a world full of pain and uncertainty.

Perhaps this soldier would have gone to the Wall and laid down his terrible guilt years earlier if he had lived with more truth, respect, and responsibility. Or perhaps because he was living with these virtues he was finally able to make his pilgrimage and not carry his pain to the grave. It is not for us to judge others. I know that when we do the best we can—and we alone are the judge of that—we take ourselves off the hook and invite grace.

Commitment is not so much a value as a series of tools that takes our values and empowers them. Our intentional love needs commitment to have it bear fruit. Our commitments take the